Published by SM-ARC, inc.,

5221 9th avenue s., st. petersburg, fl, 33707

Sm.art.ren.collab@gmail.com

www.a-view-from-the-tendo.com

ISBN-13: 978-0-9979212-0-5

Library on Congress 2016951268

A View From the Tendõ

a rumination on the rules of one man's life

by

Hitori Arukimasu

Table of contents

Forward

I am not Hitori Arukimasu; this is the name I wear when I work in Japanese calligraphy, as an expression of respect to the culture from which I borrow for these projects, and to acknowledge what I am: a man who *walks alone.* I am not Hitori Arukimasu.

I am not a beloved man. Do not mistake me: I don't offer this appraisal in search of sympathy or scorn, but merely—as with other views from the *tendō*—to give voice to one of the truths of my life. I am not a beloved man.

In a conventional life, it might be convenient to question the fairness of this, but mine is not a conventional life, & quotidian notions of fairness & convenience have no place here. The qualities I possess that help me understand the totality of things are ironically the same qualities that make me, in the words of my brother, Ansgar, "exasperating". Quite inconveniently, I would rather be exasperating & alone with my gifts—gifts the value of which I will never underestimate—than adored for my inadequacies & failures by a mob of people who squander their own gifts daily. I knew a woman once who surrounded herself with her "genius types", the only qualification for which seemed to be a surfeit of social handicaps or a low E.Q.; I was not one of her geniuses, & was gone from her life before she realized I was in it. The number of people I have left far exceeds the number of people I keep with me; to this peculiar condition every one of the tenets in this book applies.

There is no part of this book that bears any resemblance to Machiavelli, or to Nietsche, or to any of the other cynical, pessimistic existentialists whose toxic self-interest is so popularly quoted by the hip, the young, & the pretentious. The view from the Tendō is not about hipness or youngness or pretentions, cynicism or pessimism: I am an optimist, & often naïve, which comes with its own costs, but at least not at the expense of my conscience, which seems so to me of far greater value.

I live a life in search of knowledge & experience. This life has led me to some fascinating discoveries, not all of which are mine, but all of which have profited me nonetheless. What I share in the pages that follow are a few of the rules with which I organize that life: the tenets of my existence. They are aspirational; they are mine. You, the reader, may find rules here that appeal to your own sensibilities, or apply to your own circumstances, but you are not me: some of my rules may have no relevance for you at all. I encourage you to make your own rules, create your own temple of mind where you can aspire to be the best version of yourself. Study & learn new things, so that your temple may be vast. Eschew the petty thoughts and gossips that distract you from your temple. Discipline yourself in thinking, so that, even when all prevaricating ideologies count you as wrong, you remain the voice of truth. Be unafraid of revealing that truth: your life is not a popularity contest; it is a quest for knowledge & experience, which may leave you, like me, to *walk alone*, but I assure you that road is never lonely.

There are people whose contributions to my life it pleases me to acknowledge. Abstractly, I must thank Sei Shōnagon, Miyamoto Musashi, Rumi, & Kahlil Gibran for inspiring this book: they, too, made lists, ruminated on truths, cherished the beauty of language—or just the beauty of beauty—and inspired me with the messages they sent into their futures. My father, whose name I do not use, taught me to embrace rejection & to enjoy my own company; my stepfather, Fred G. Schork, who is my real father, possessed a deep and patient wisdom, & taught me to endure love; they are both gone, but they, too, sent messages into their futures, and speak from inside me. Arthur Satz, Stephen Jay Gould, & Edward Sedlmeier showed me how to seek truth & honesty, how to discipline my mind, how to be a coherent custodian of knowledge, & how to share it eloquently. My late wife, Mary, who found me in her classroom, helped me cultivate my voice until the way I spoke & wrote precisely mirrored the way I thought & felt. There are many others to whom I owe gratitude, but I'll conclude with my mother, Carol Schork, who, when I was a boy, transformed my world with magic that has never left me, and who, in my adulthood, has taught me more than she realizes, about implacable courage & resilience, and the fierceness of loyalty & love. These are some of my teachers…

–Hitori Arukimasu

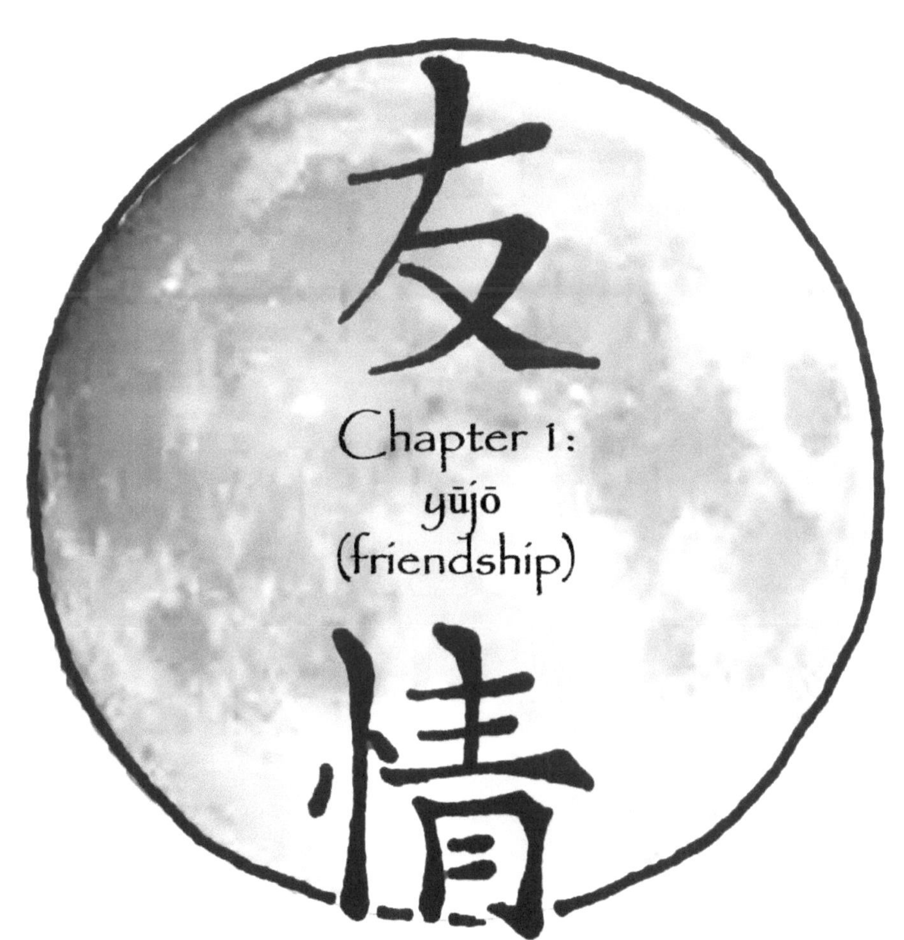
友
Chapter 1:
yūjō
(friendship)
情

Friendship, part 1:

"Having a few right friends is better than having many wrong friends."

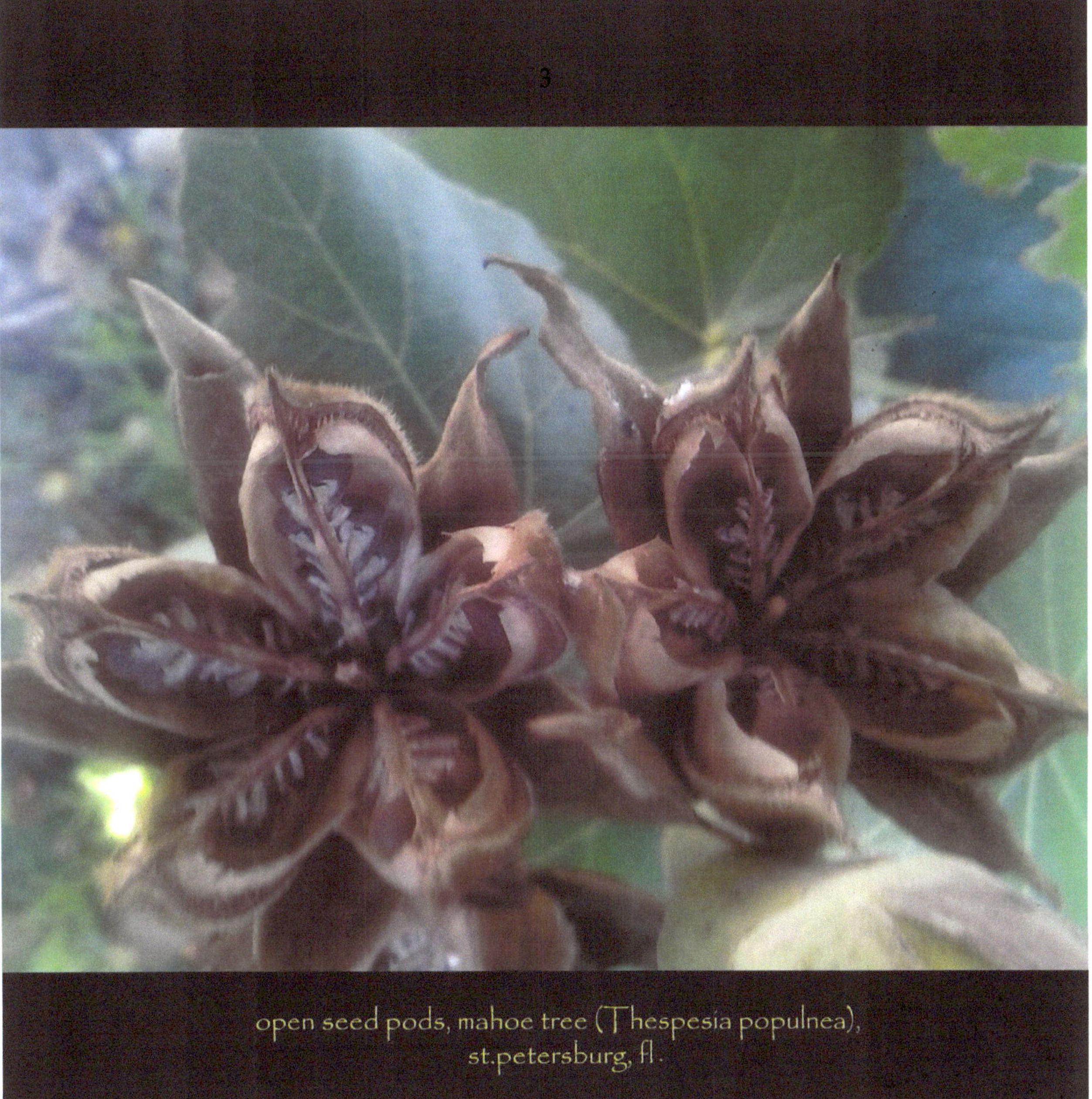

open seed pods, mahoe tree (Thespesia populnea),
st.petersburg, fl.

Friendship, part 2:

"Having one friend who will speak the truth to you

is better than having a hundred friends

who will tell you what they think you want to hear."

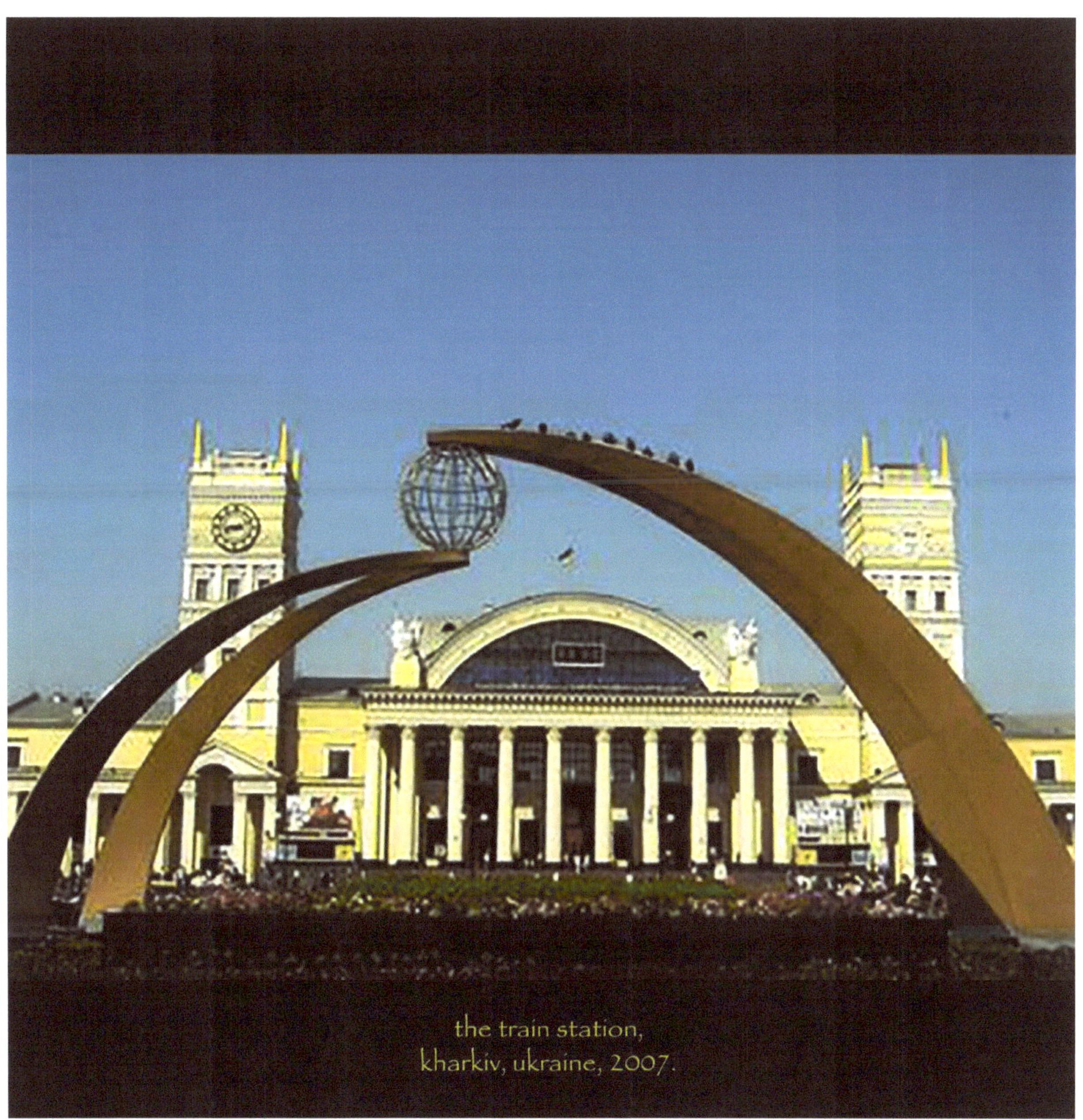

the train station,
kharkiv, ukraine, 2007.

A meeting on the road~

Creeping slowly away from the headstones & monuments
Of failed acquaintance,
Only to encounter again—and delightfully—
The smile of a friend who overtook me on my way,

I think...

I think...

And upon the impossible scope & breadth
Of distance,
Marvel at the loyalty of the hand
In which my own hand lay...

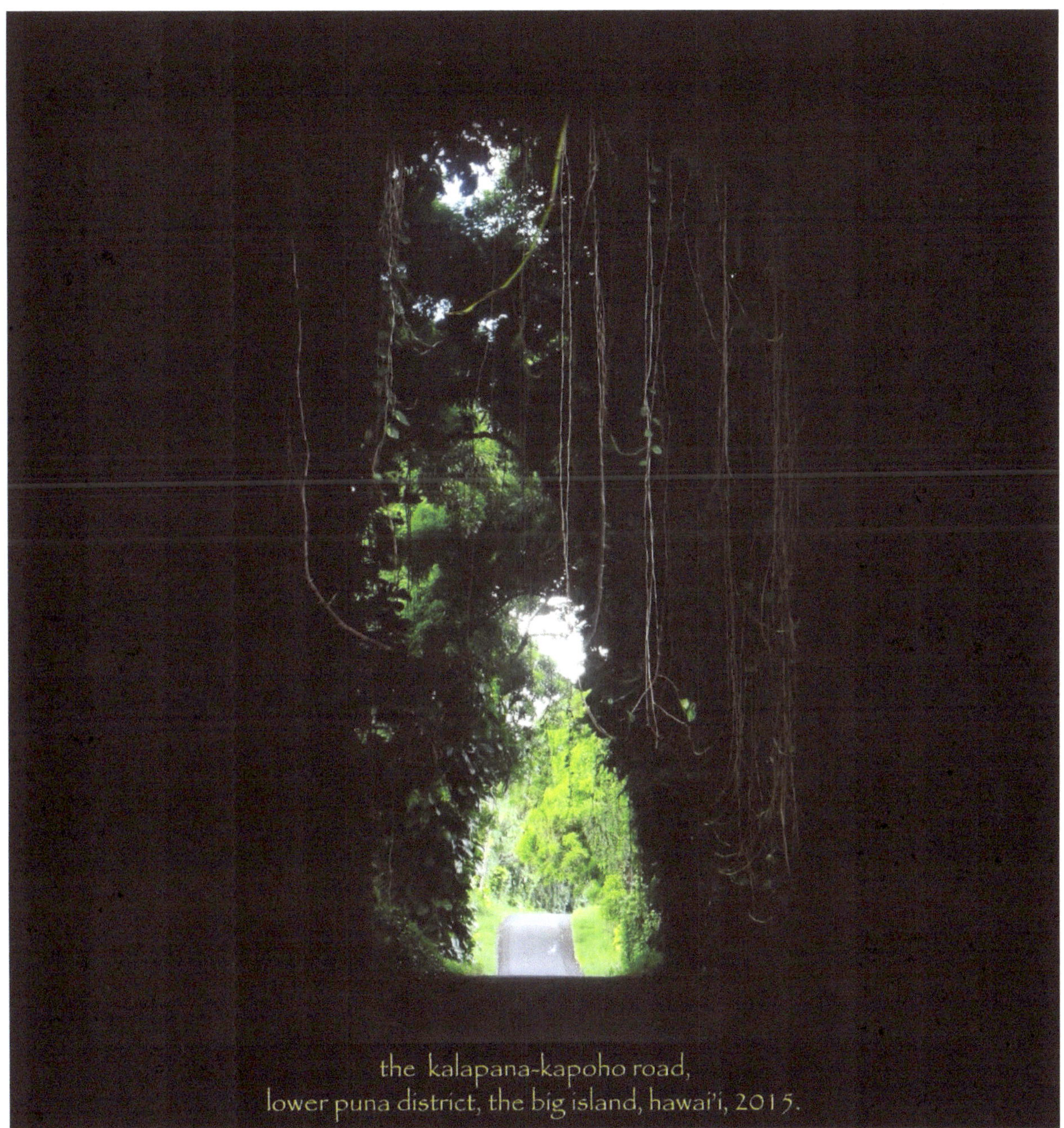

the kalapana-kapoho road,
lower puna district, the big island, hawai'i, 2015.

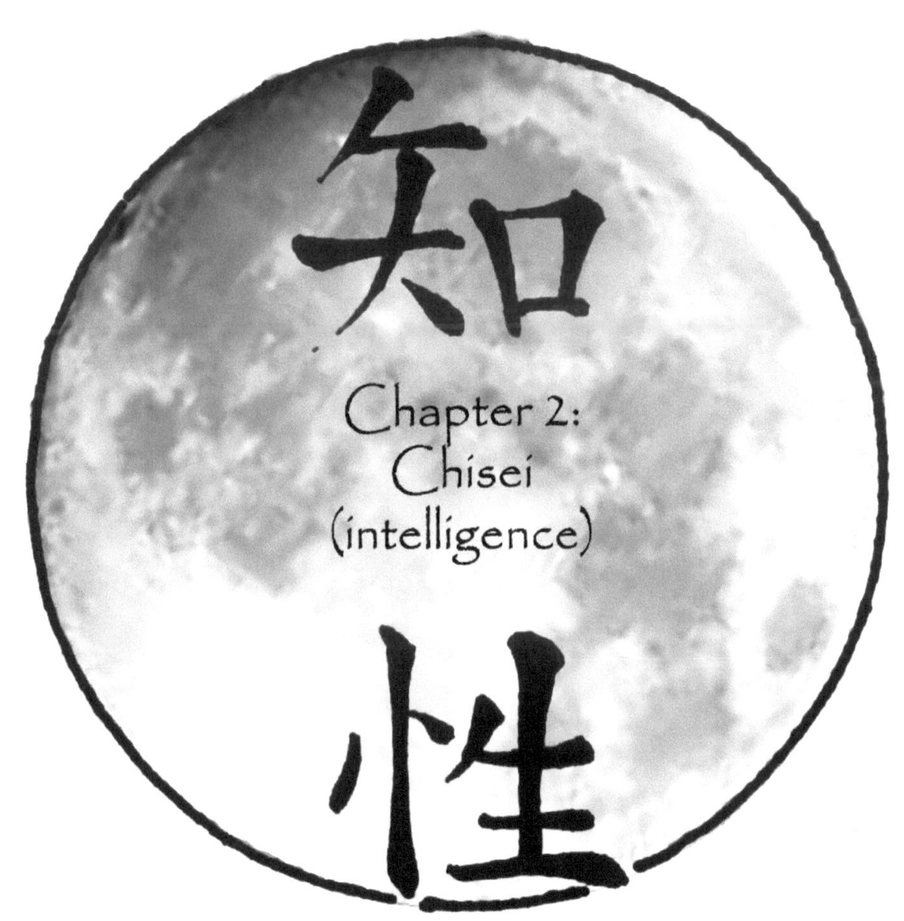
知
Chapter 2:
Chisei
(intelligence)
性

Intelligence, part 1:

"Being the smartest person in the room

will not make you the most popular person in the room."

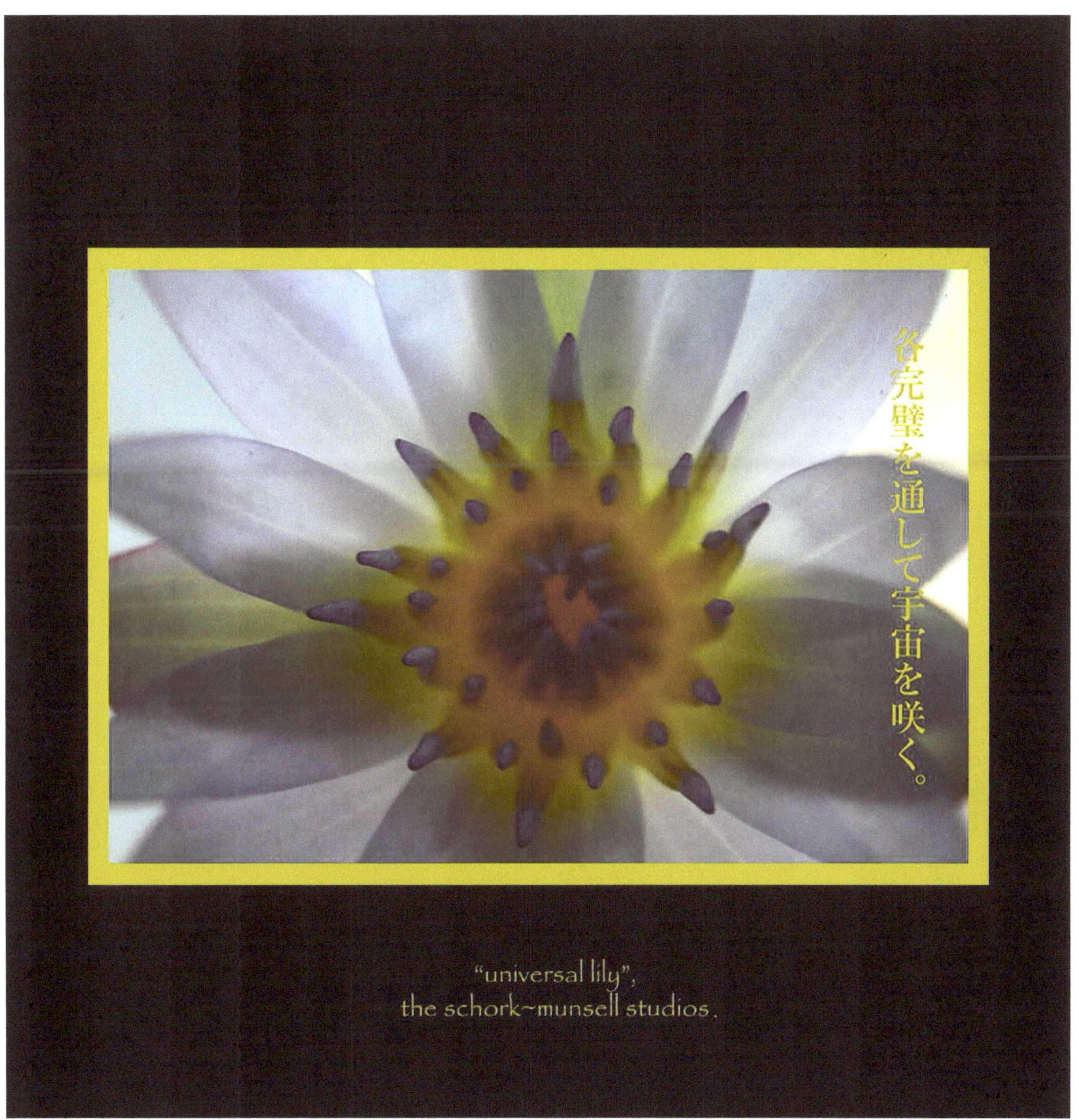

"universal lily",
the schork~munsell studios.

Intelligence, part 2:

"Being the smartest person in the room

is better than being the most popular person in the room."

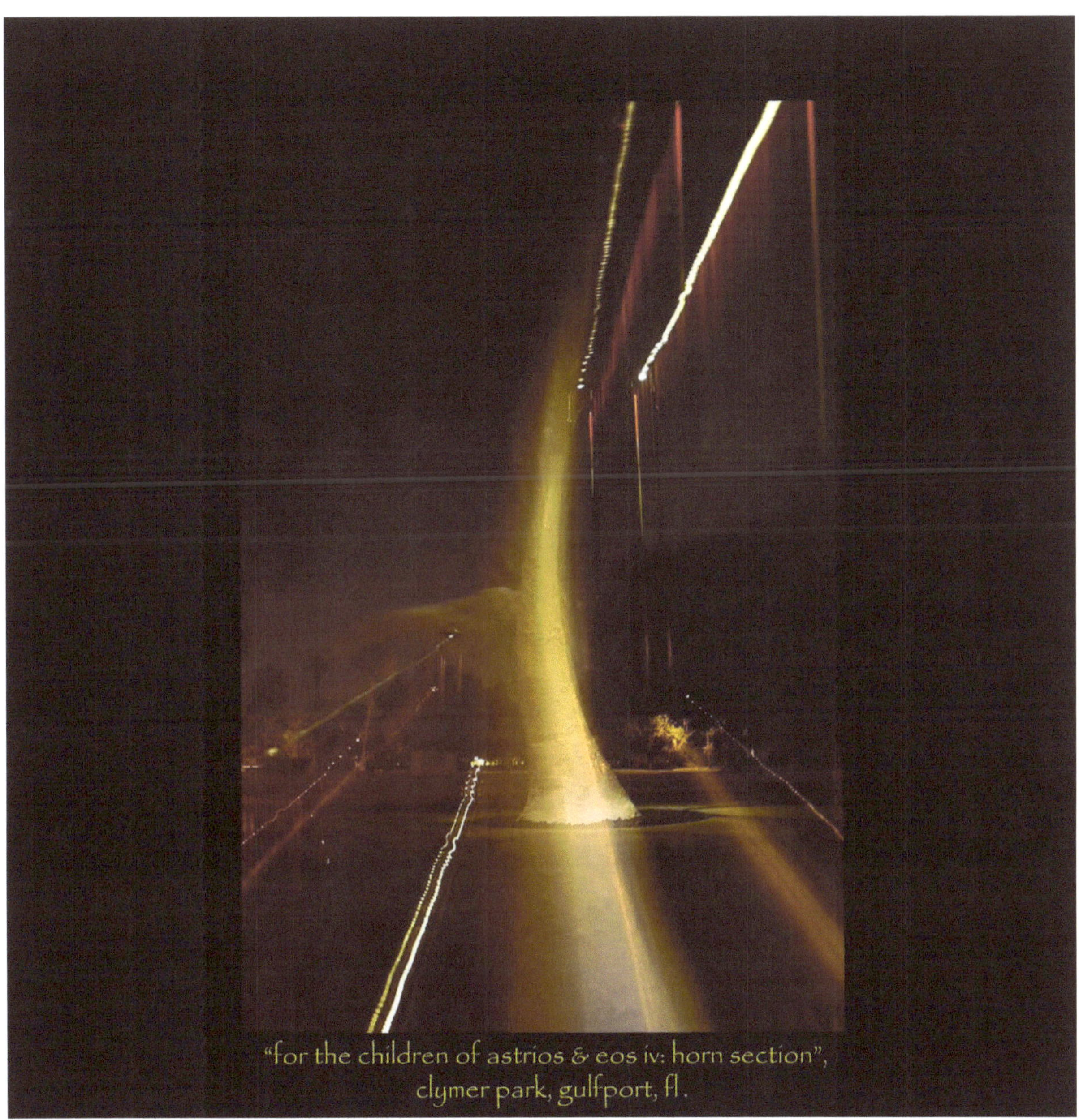

"for the children of astrios & eos iv: horn section",
clymer park, gulfport, fl.

It is an unfortunate truism that in the U.S.

intelligence is feared & scorned,

& our smartest children are bullied by our dumbest.

It is karma

that our smartest children grow into our smartest adults,

who invent the world in which everyone else lives.

Two centuries ago, our colonial intelligentsia created a nation;

today our scientists, mathematicians, artists, & engineers

lead us to the stars...

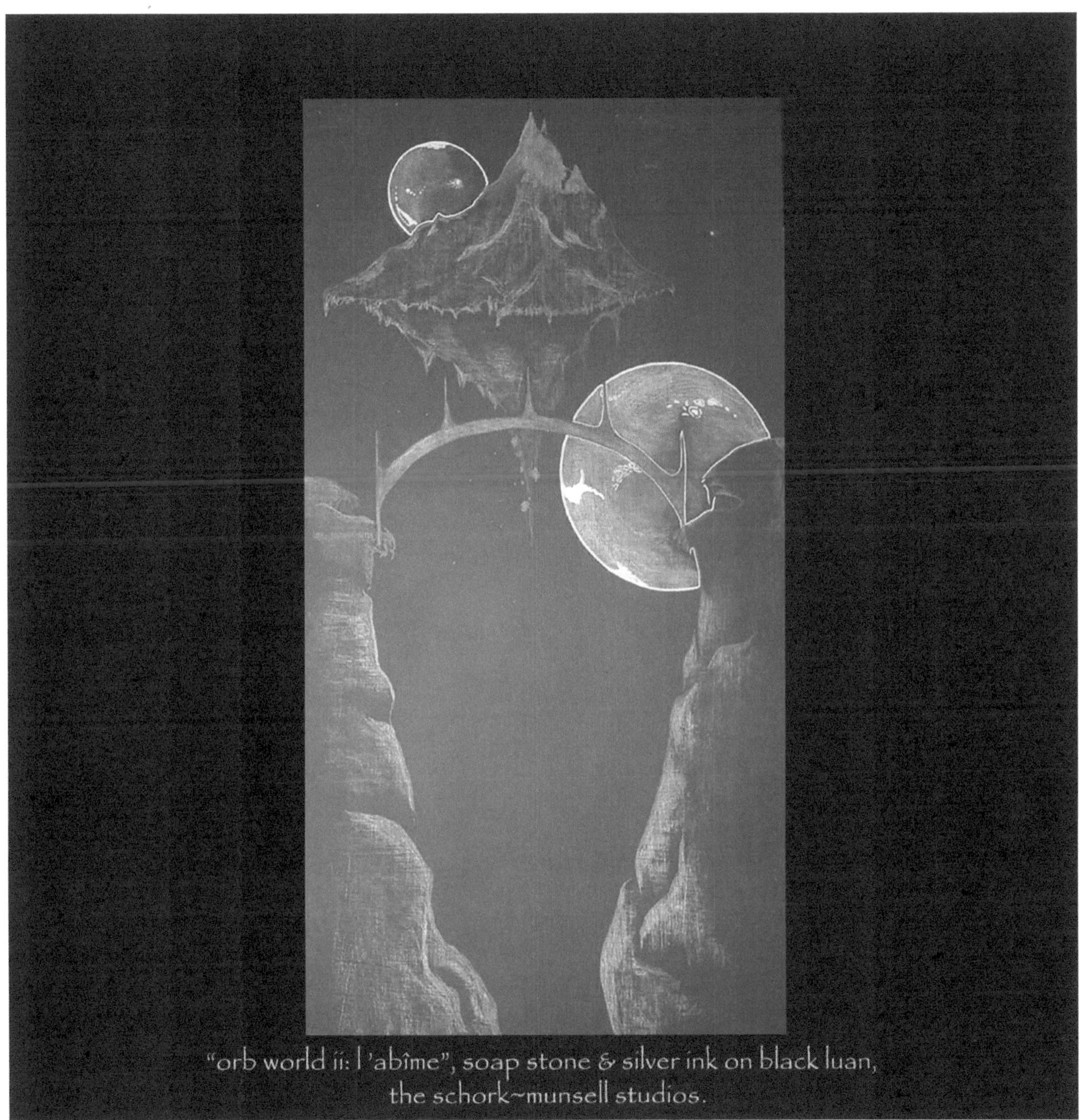

"orb world ii: l 'abîme", soap stone & silver ink on black luan,
the schork~munsell studios.

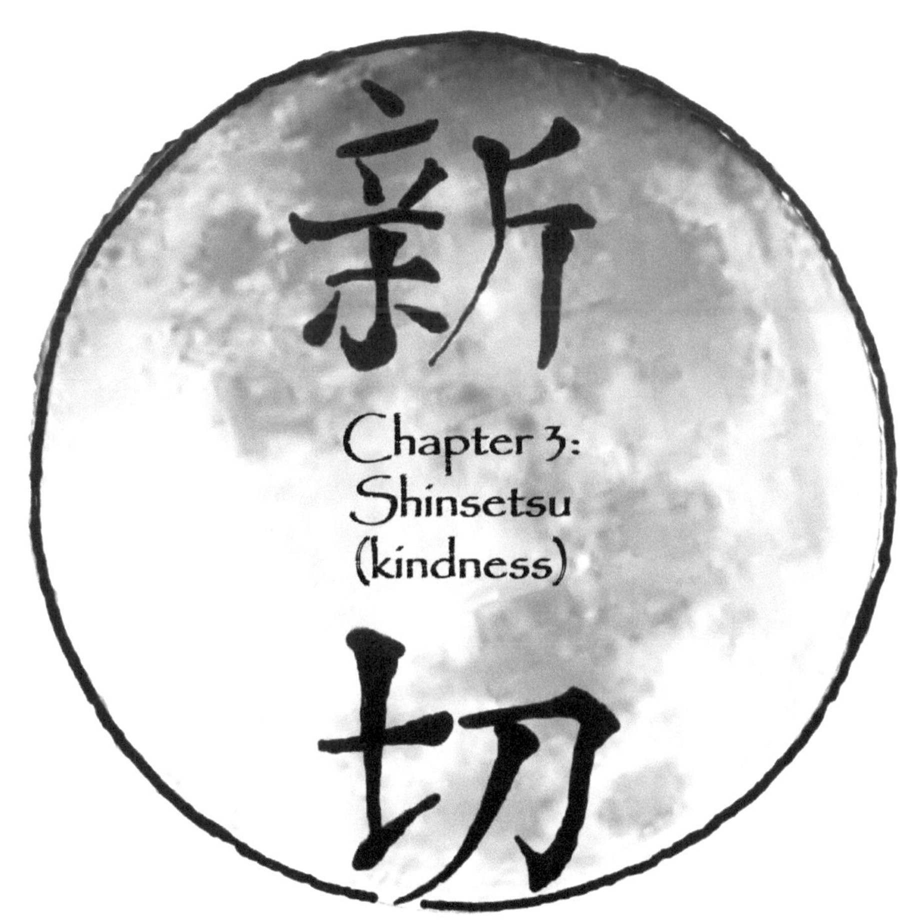
新
Chapter 3:
Shinsetsu
(kindness)
切

Kindness, part 1:

"Being a nice person does not guarantee
that you will be treated like a nice person."

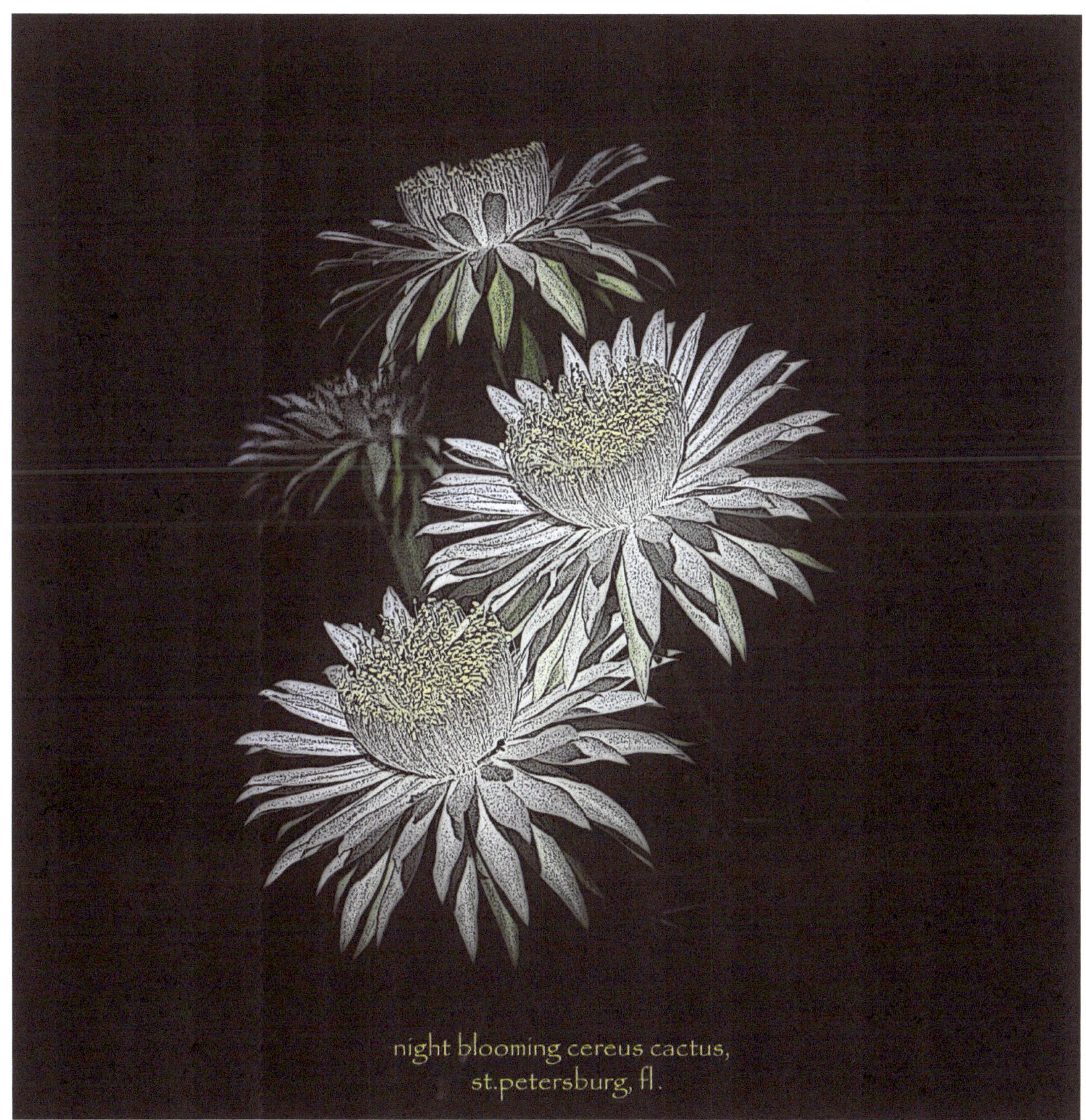

night blooming cereus cactus,
st.petersburg, fl.

Kindness, Part 2:

"Be one anyhow."

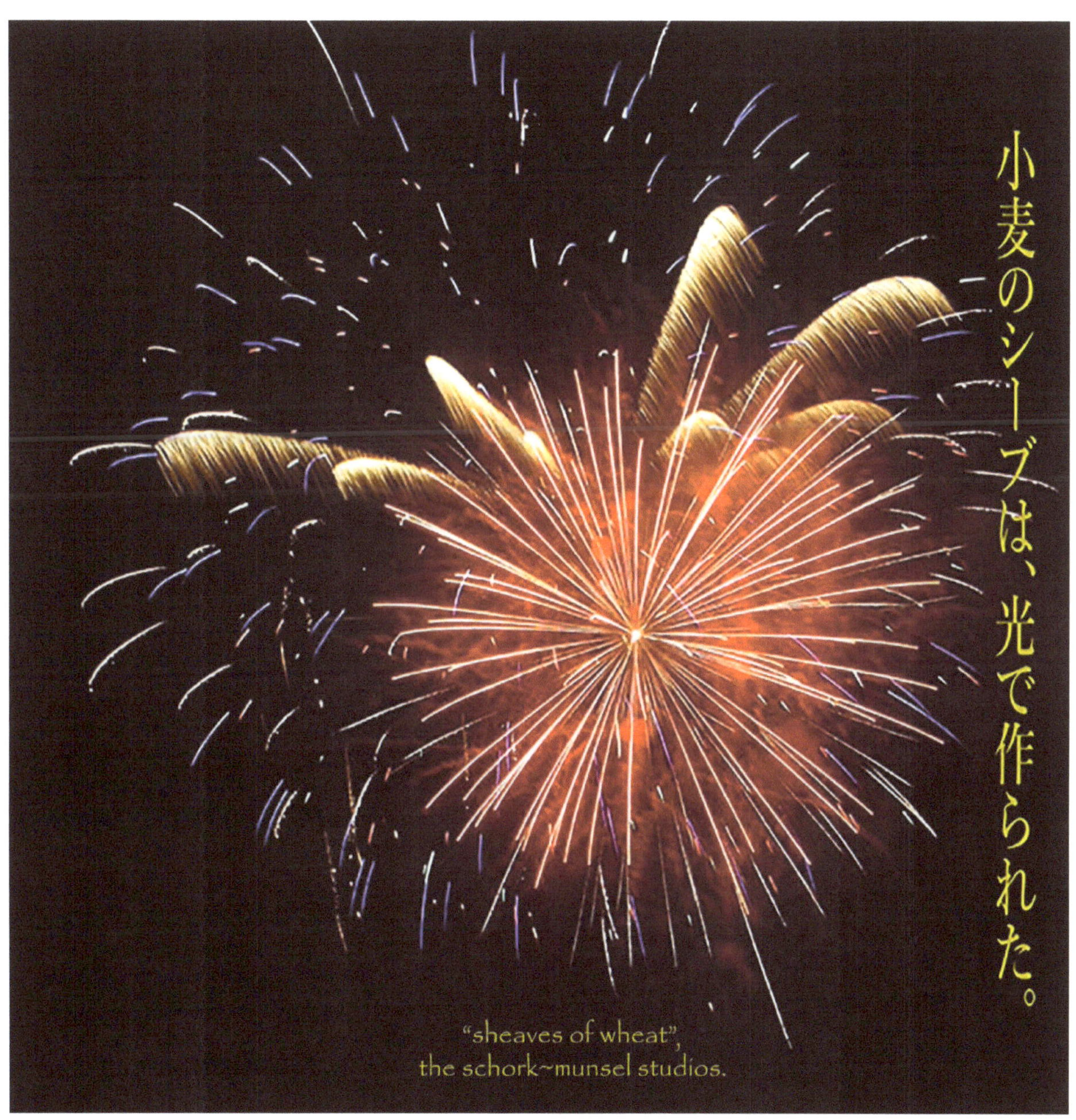

"sheaves of wheat",
the schork~munsel studios.

The Dreaming Man

He feels more real when he dreams than he feels awake.

Here, awake, he is a stranger among people who see him but do not recognize him: he is a silhouette, moving against some brilliant light that removes from him all detail—he is a shadow in the wayang.

The people he touches recoil, stung—the invisible hand, so electric & dangerous, is his hand: like animals semi-tame & desperate they take food from his fingers and retreat a hasty distance, confident of the threat they cannot possibly know. They tremble at the reflection they see in the pupils of his soul—the great, black windows of infinity they want to be but are not. Here, awake,
he is alone.

But dreaming is a far-off country, where the light is not too bright. I hear his voice like a whisper, or a thunder within: *je suis moi, mais d'autres aussie: beaucoup de gens jai revé.*

He wades across the river of time ankle deep & pauses to stoop and pass his fingers through the rill of tears… tears of joy at his return, for he is back where he belongs, in the world of dreams, however briefly.

He is home.

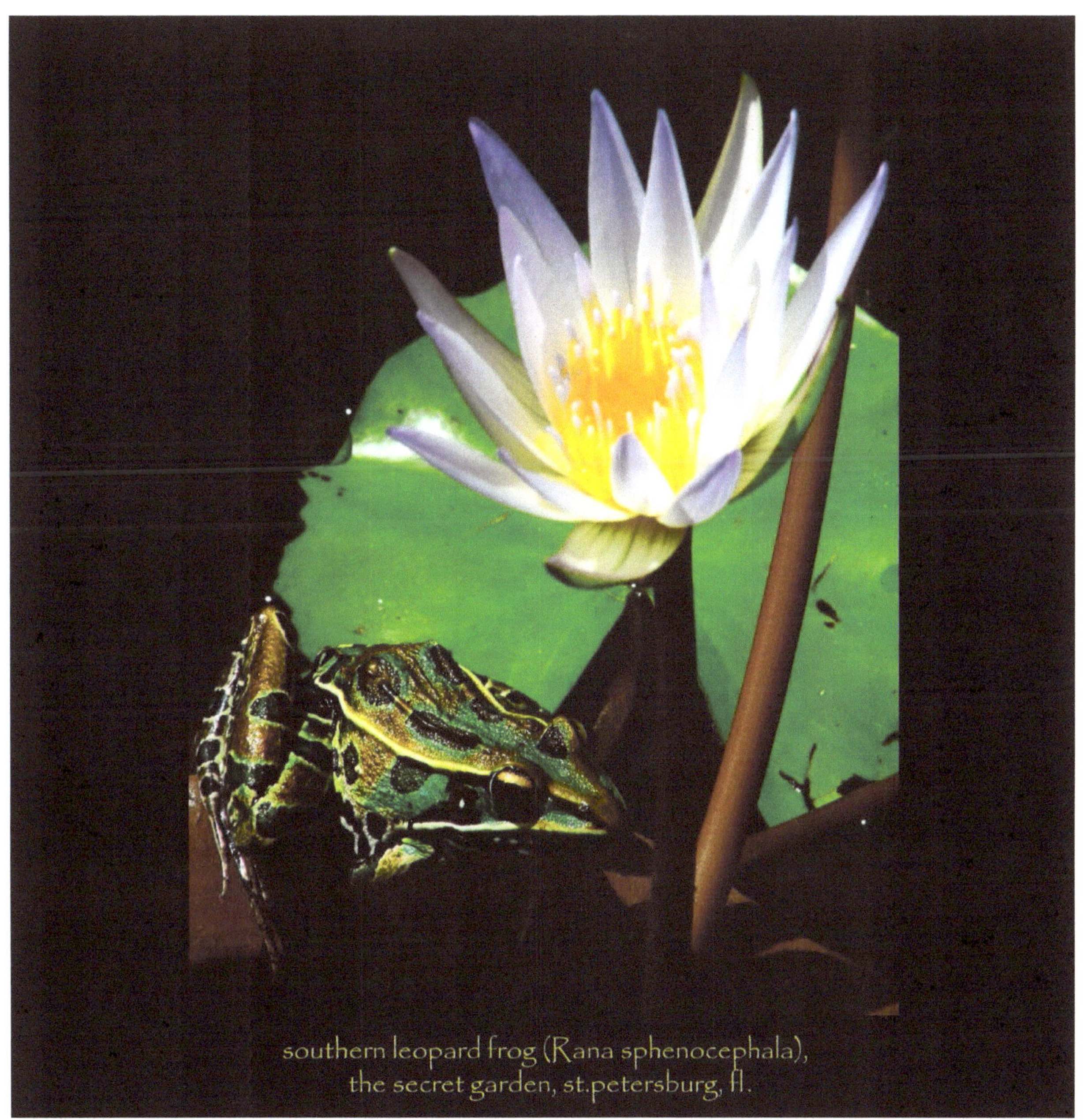

southern leopard frog (Rana sphenocephala),
the secret garden, st.petersburg, fl.

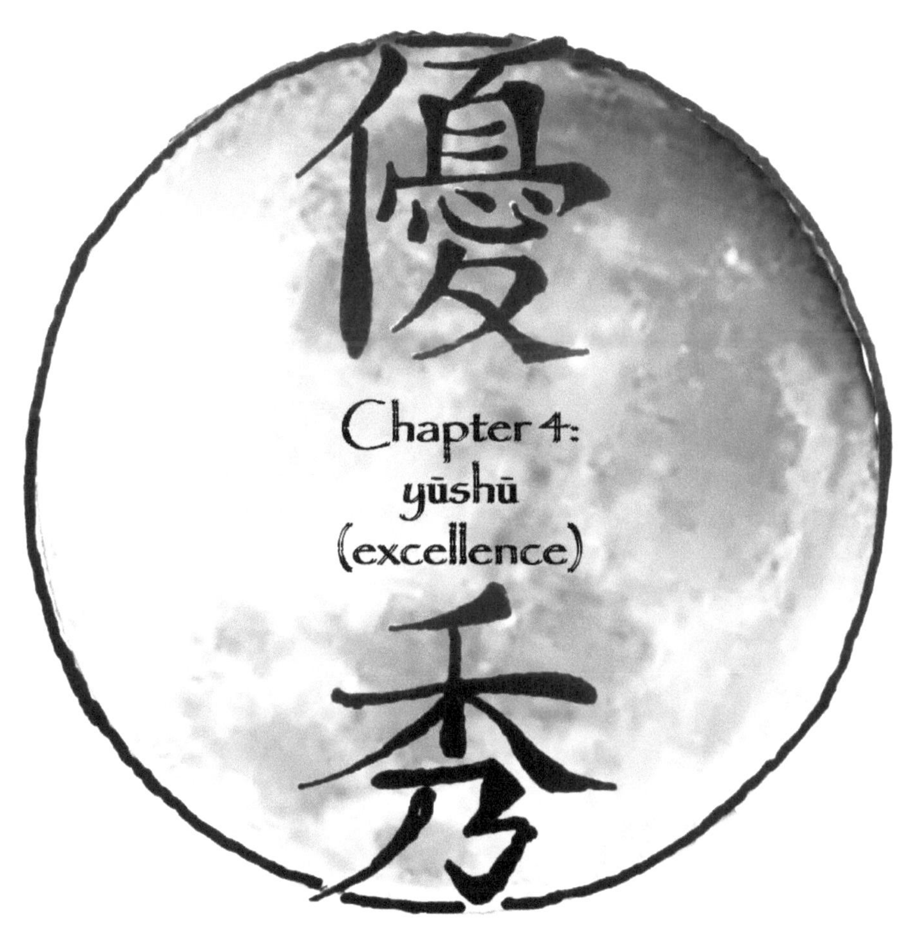
優
Chapter 4:
yūshū
(excellence)
秀

Excellence, part 1:

"Being surrounded by mediocrities is no excuse for being one."

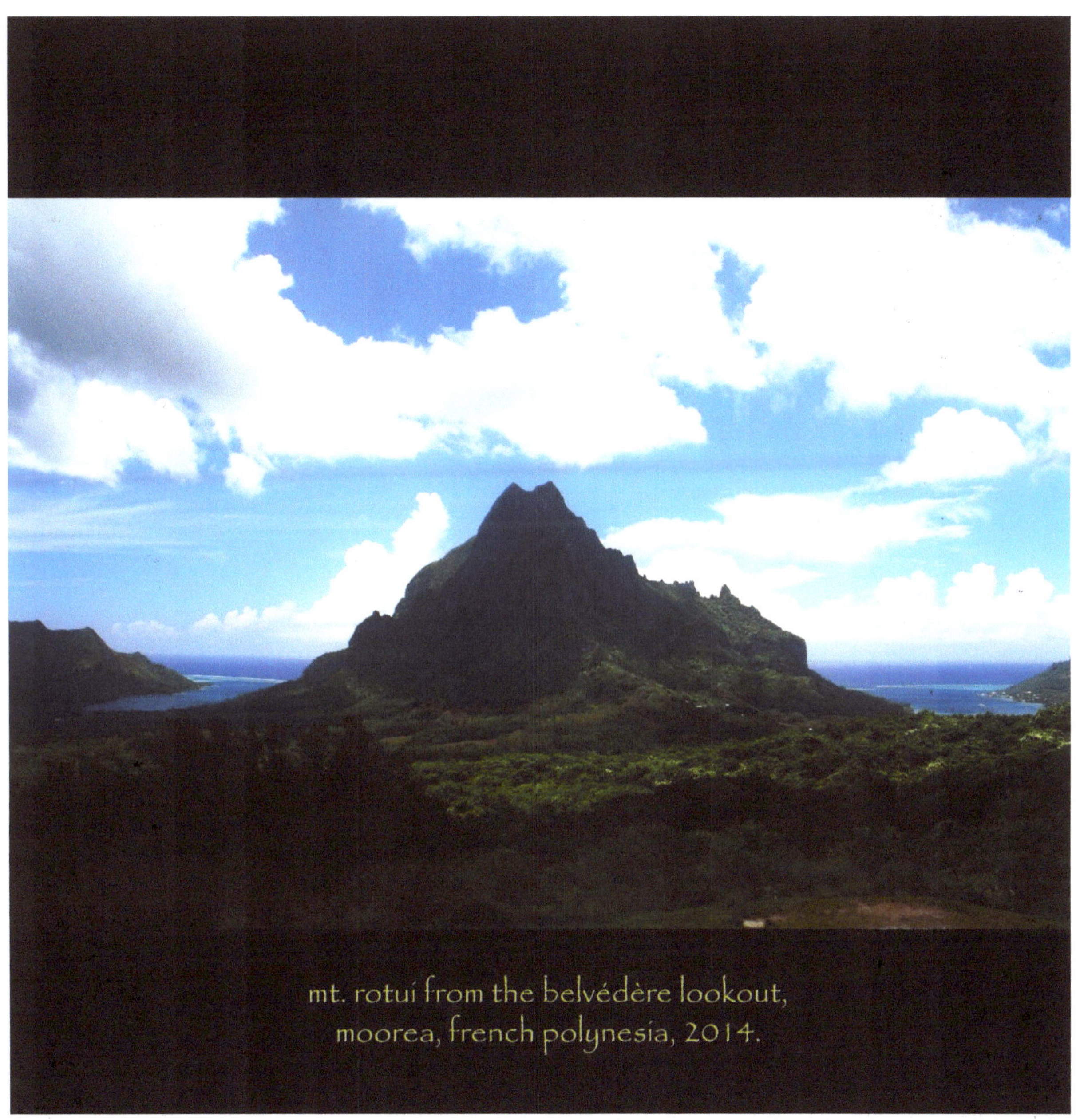

mt. rotui from the belvédère lookout,
moorea, french polynesia, 2014.

Excellence, part 2:

"Excellence is a quality, not a quantity."

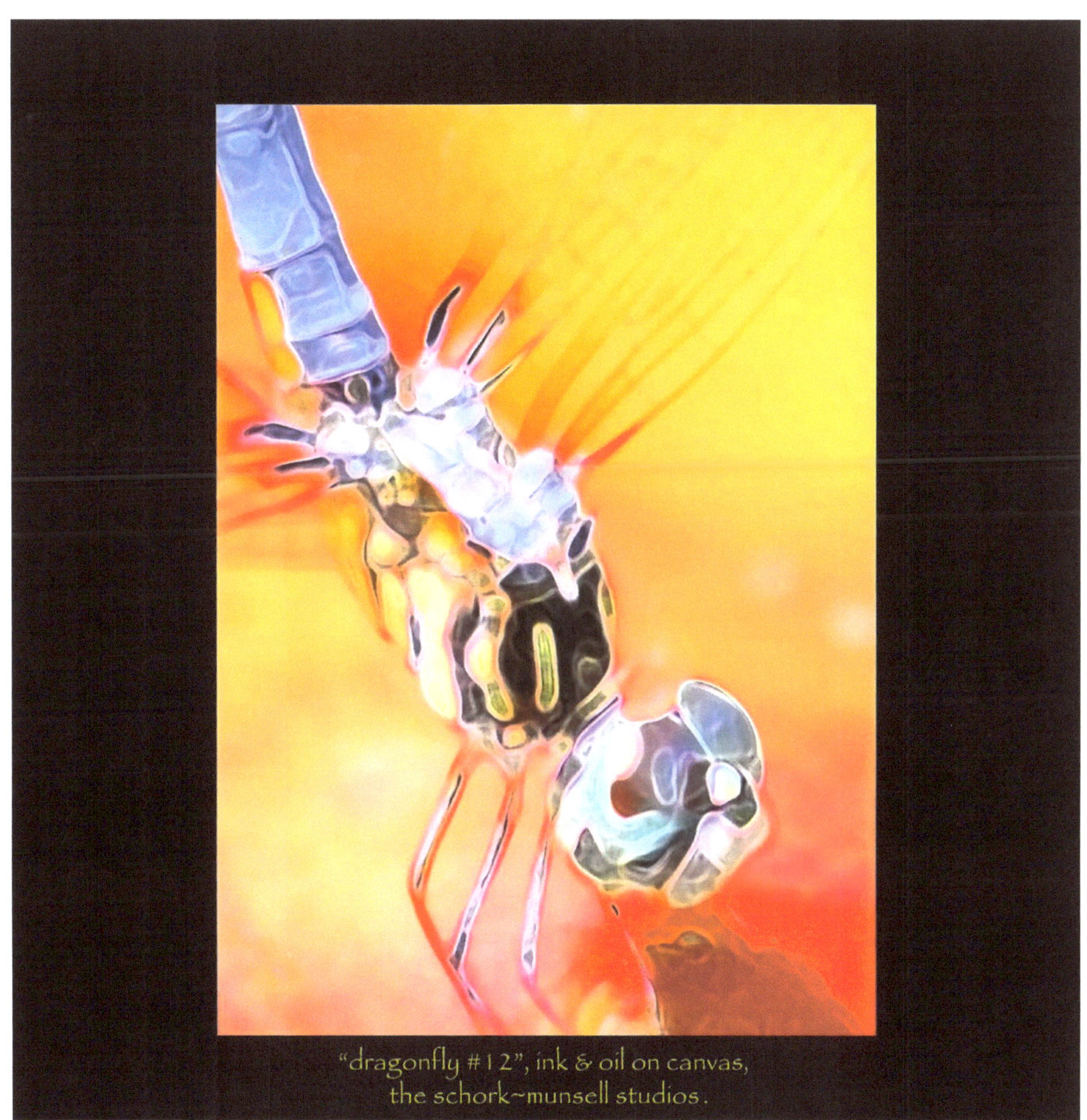

"dragonfly #12", ink & oil on canvas,
the schork~munsell studios.

память ~

осень песня вчера,

когда мы были большими и зеленый и высокий,

но наш блеск наша последняя мелодия:

осень песня падения...

(memory~

autumn is a song of yesterday,

when we were great & green & tall,

but our brilliance is our last melody:

autumn is a song of the fall...)

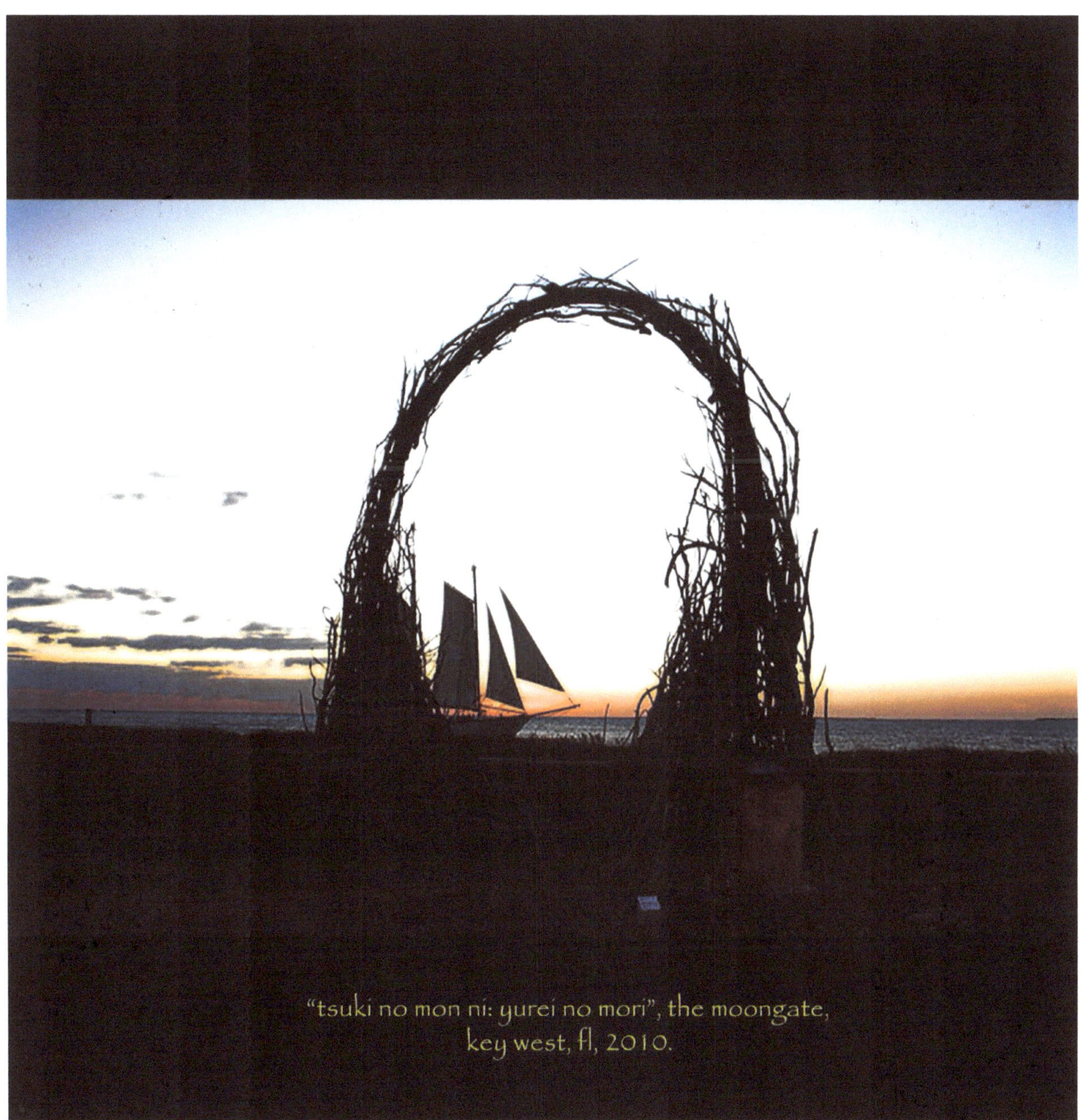

"tsuki no mon ni: yurei no mori", the moongate,
key west, fl, 2010.

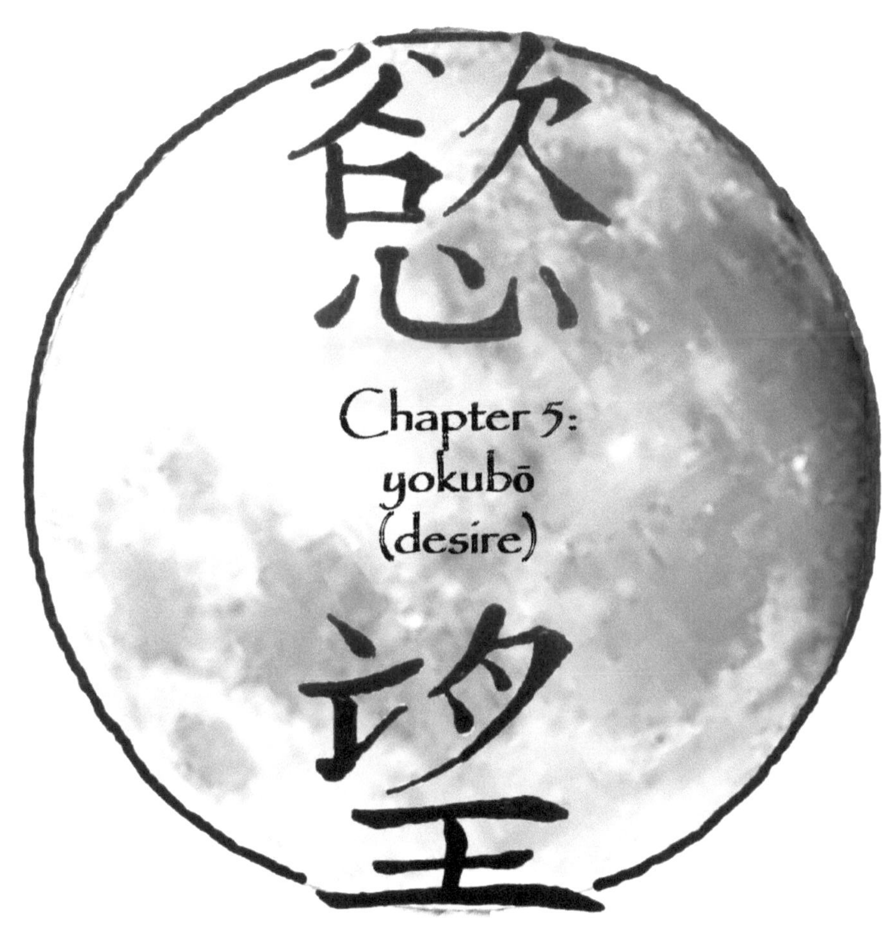

Chapter 5: yokubō (desire)

Desire, part 1:

"There is a difference between 'need' & 'want'."

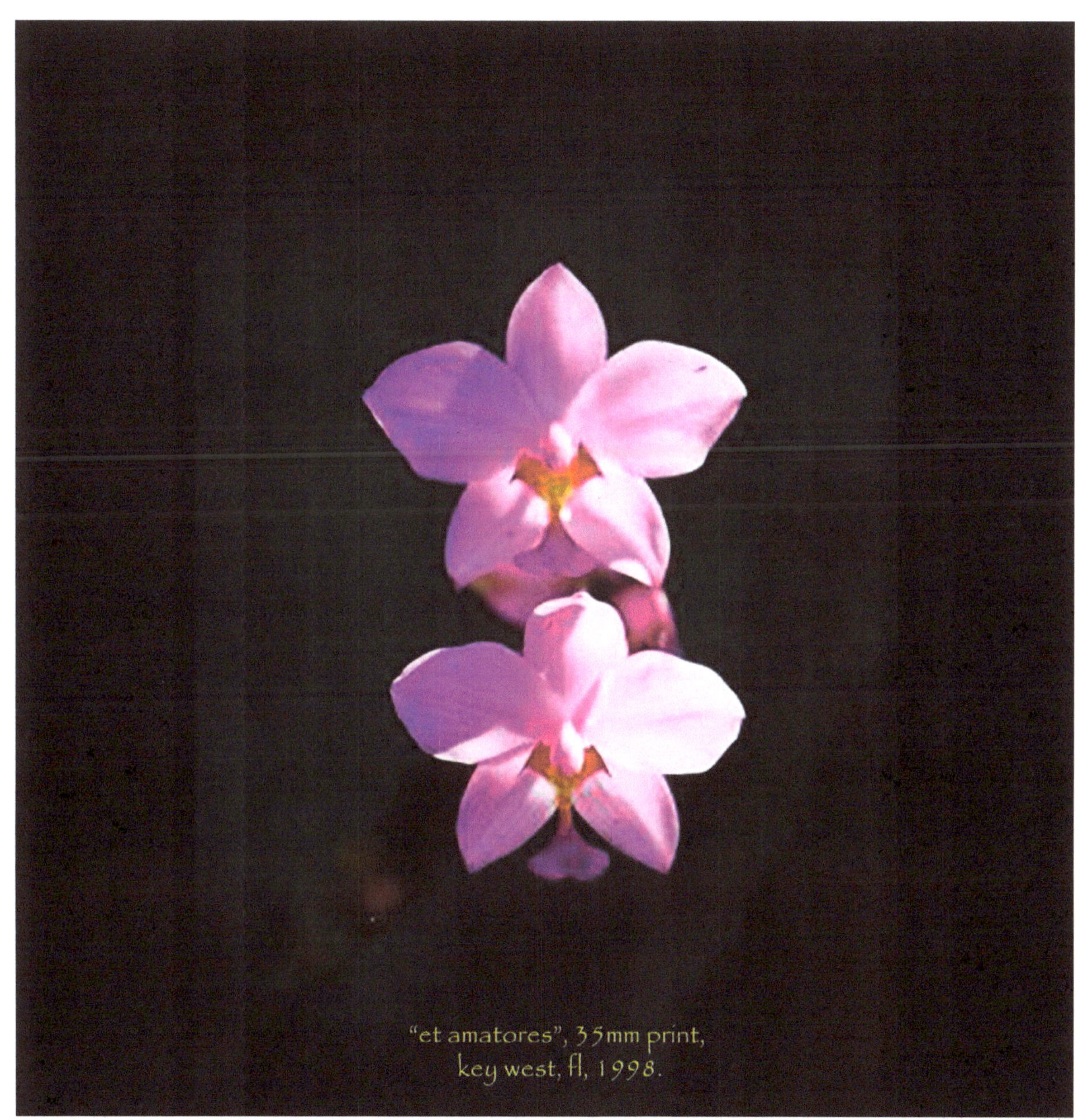

"et amatores", 35mm print,
key west, fl, 1998.

Desire, part 2:

"It is excellent to know the difference."

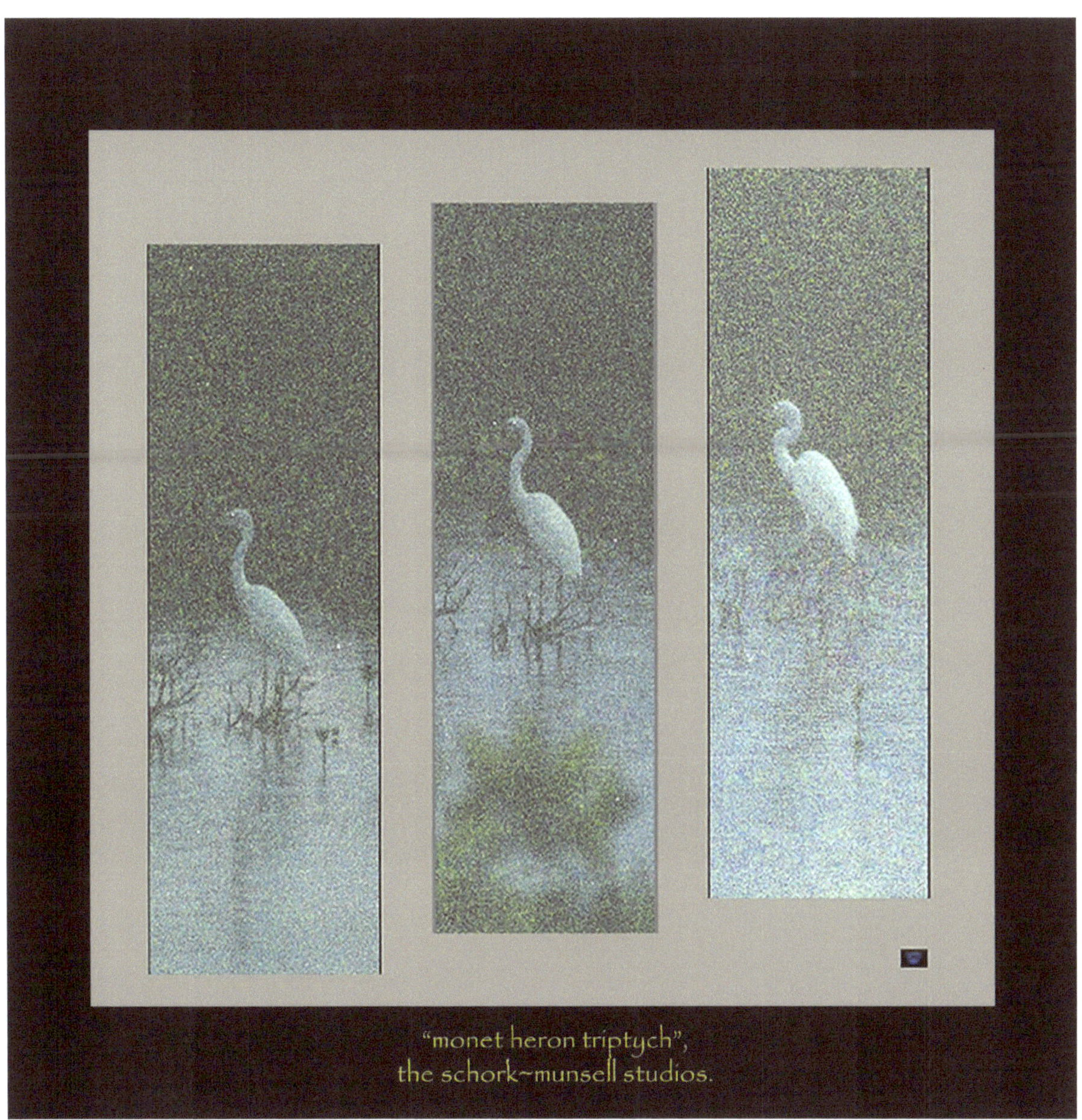

"monet heron triptych",
the schork~munsell studios.

"All is clouded by desire, Arjuna,

As a fire by smoke,

As a mirror by dust.

Through these, it blinds the soul."

Billy Kwan, *The Year of Living Dangerously*

(quoting the *Bhagavad Gita*)

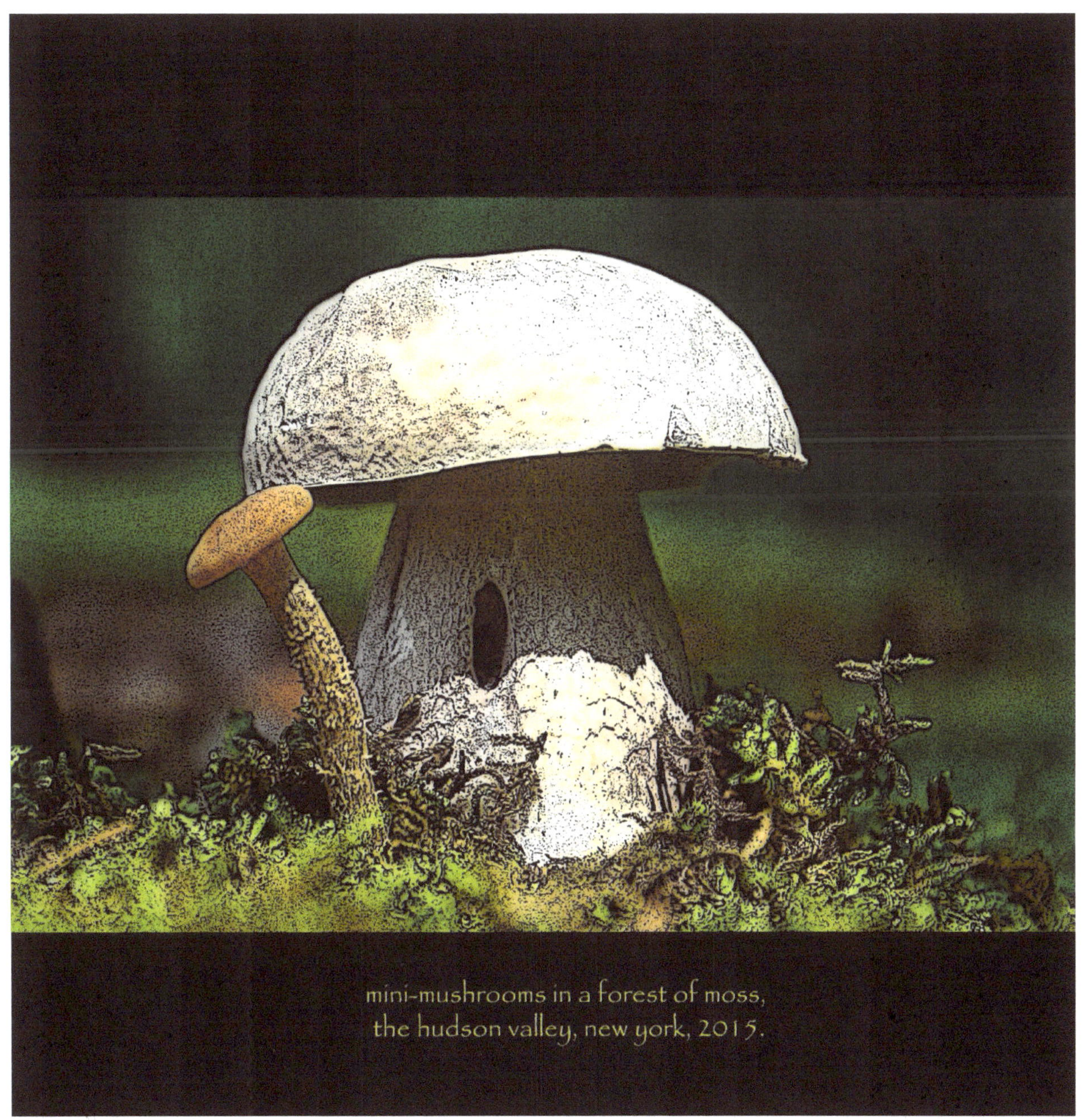

mini-mushrooms in a forest of moss,
the hudson valley, new york, 2015.

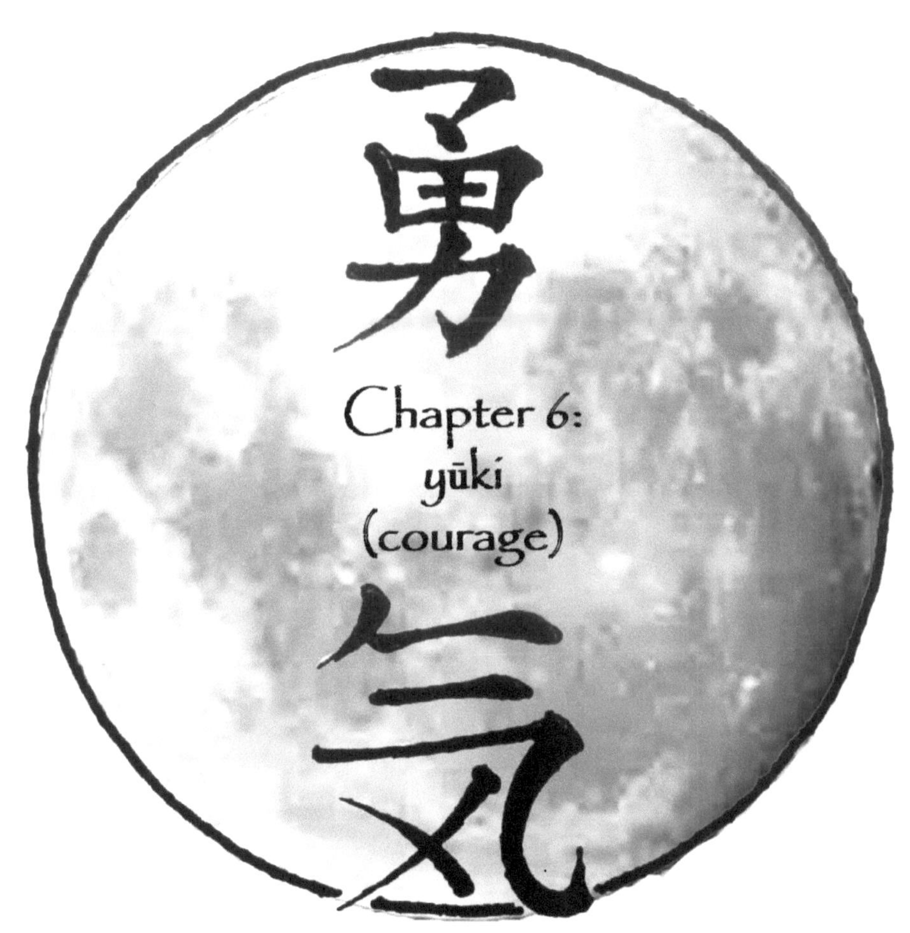
勇
Chapter 6:
yūki
(courage)
気

Courage, part 1:

"Fear is the worst reason to do something, or not to do something."

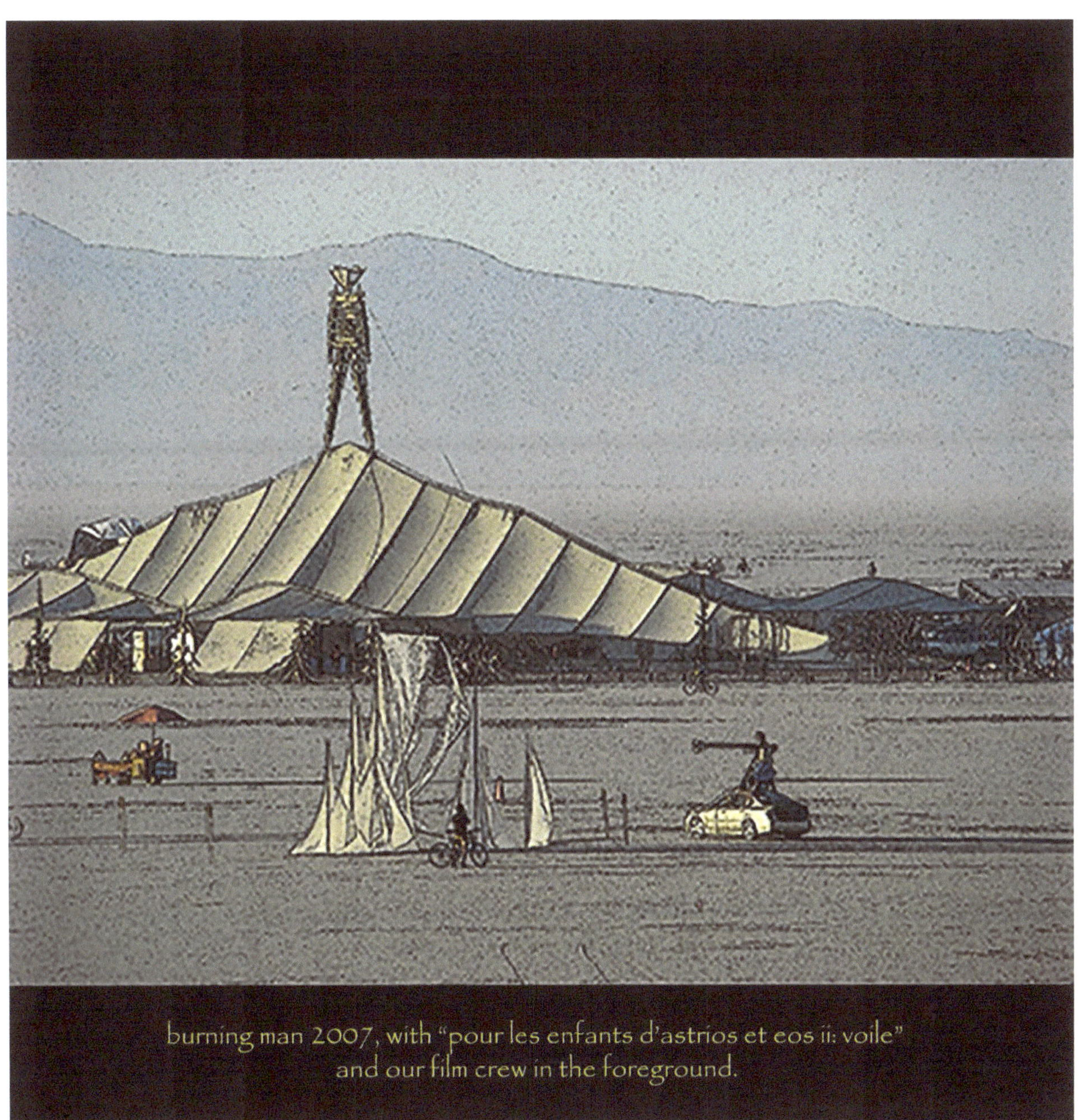

burning man 2007, with "pour les enfants d'astrios et eos ii: voile" and our film crew in the foreground.

Courage, part 2:

"Fearful people live longer, but not really."

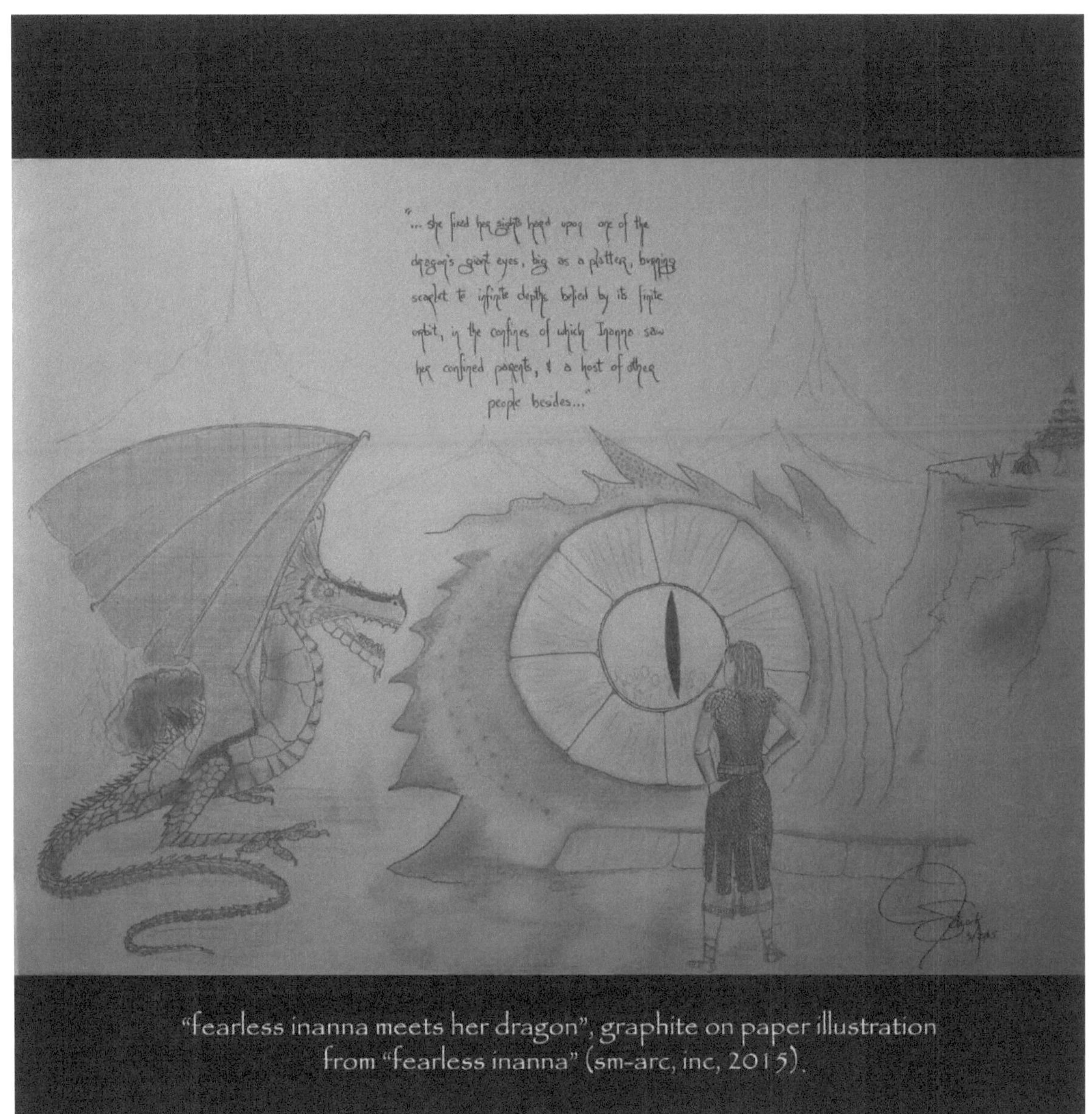

"fearless inanna meets her dragon", graphite on paper illustration from "fearless inanna" (sm-arc, inc, 2015).

What happened to us?

When I was a little boy, I thought I was afraid of heights. I would leap off the roof of the house in an attempt to challenge my fear, to fix it, and to a certain extent it worked: I gradually discovered that what I was really afraid of was not heights at all—it was falling. This is a defining characteristic of fear: we are seldom afraid of what we think we are afraid of.

If I wanted to muse on fear in an earnest or sincere way I might invoke Churchill & Roosevelt—the former inspired his nation to courage; the latter dragged his reluctant country into heroism—but fear is too ridiculous to dignify with such sentiments.

The U.S. has become a timid nation. Too many people are afraid of their neighbors, afraid of failure, afraid of success, afraid of the world, afraid of life. How can we possibly accomplish anything significant if we allow ourselves to be distracted from what's important by who's in the bathroom stall next to us? Is your religion really so paltry that you need special favours to protect it? Is a lone black man honestly so terrifying you need six law enforcement officers with guns drawn to subdue him, so often lately relegating him to the body bag because it's simply more convenient to shoot first and ask questions later? Why are we more afraid of losing our cars than our planet?

Biochemically, fearful people are swimming in cortisol, a hormone of stress. When we had to escape actual predators—lions & tigers & bears, oh my—cortisol had its uses: it permitted us to react more swiftly, with greater physical strength & speed, but it has its costs: anxiety, depression, insomnia, hypertension, neuroticism. Once, we were prey & afraid for a reason; now we're just afraid, and no one's jumping off the roof to find out of what or why.

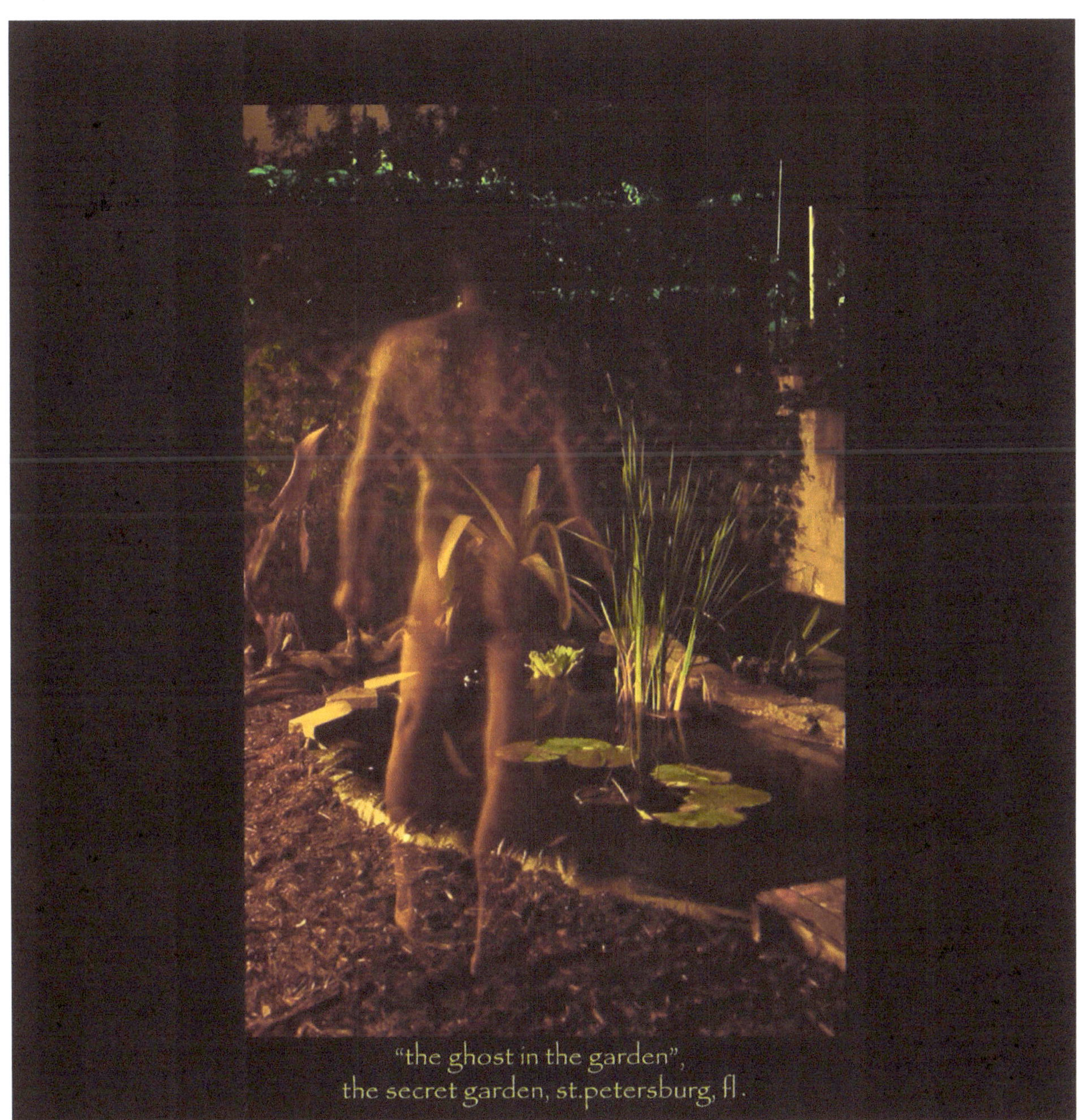
"the ghost in the garden",
the secret garden, st.petersburg, fl.

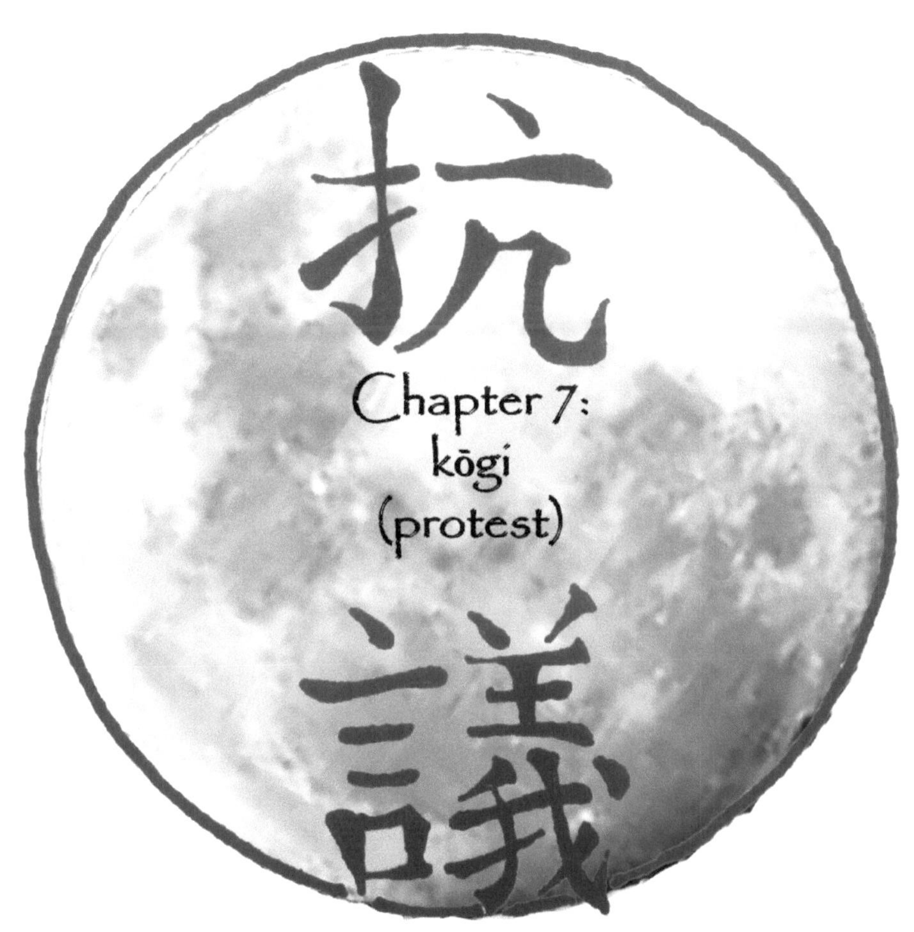
抗
Chapter 7:
kōgi
(protest)
議

Protest, part 1:

"To witness a transgression & say nothing

is to participate in that transgression."

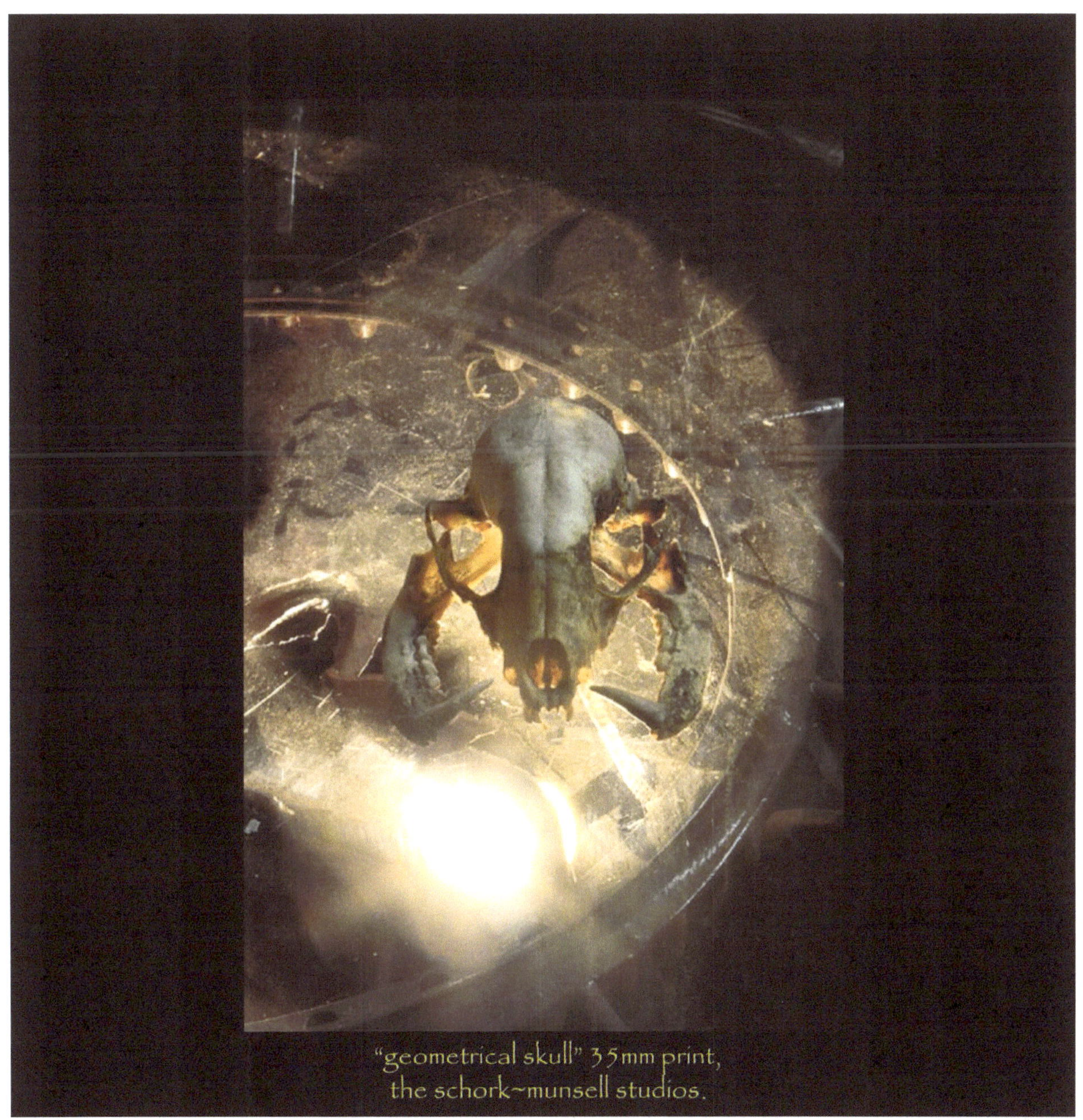

"geometrical skull" 35mm print,
the schork~munsell studios.

Protest, part 2:

"The cost of protesting a transgression is often dear;

the cost of failing to protest is always far greater."

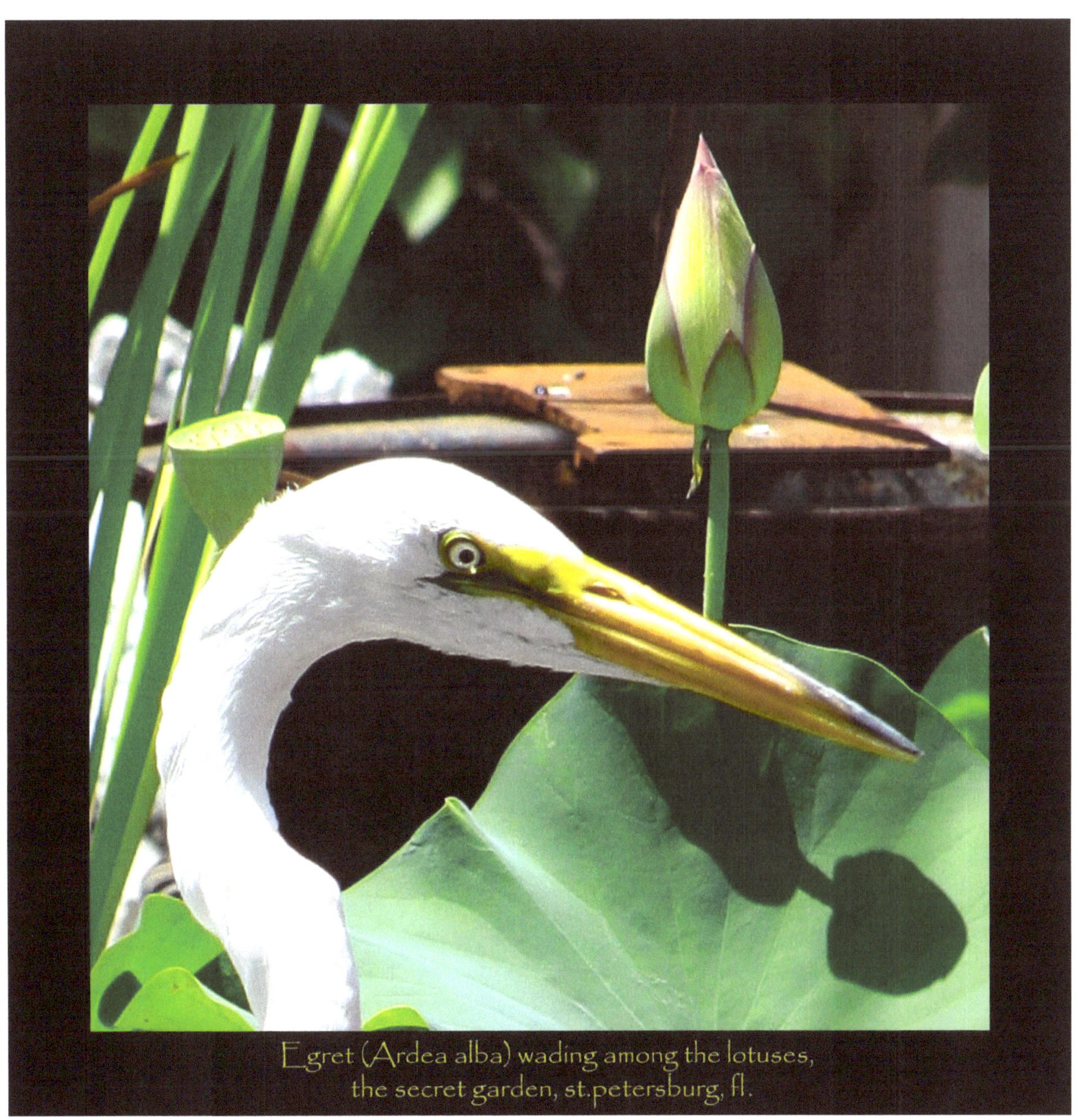

Egret (Ardea alba) wading among the lotuses,
the secret garden, st.petersburg, fl.

The Coward~

Lost in the desert, I thirsted unto death. On Lethe's banks at last I mused:

drink & heedless save my life, or take my mem'ries with me?

An angel then there was who looked like Poe: forlorn, he handed me a cup.

I think I drank from this, he told me, *but I do not know.*

Behind me the crooked teeth of the desert bend into a grin,

the sands spilling down as from an hourglass, each grain one less breath of me.

The last moa had come this way & the last dodo, doomed:

with courage they stared back into the wastes and lost with them all their ancient tribe.

But I am a human being: courage has long forsaken us.

I will drain that cup: I will save myself and drown a litany of misdeeds...

Again...

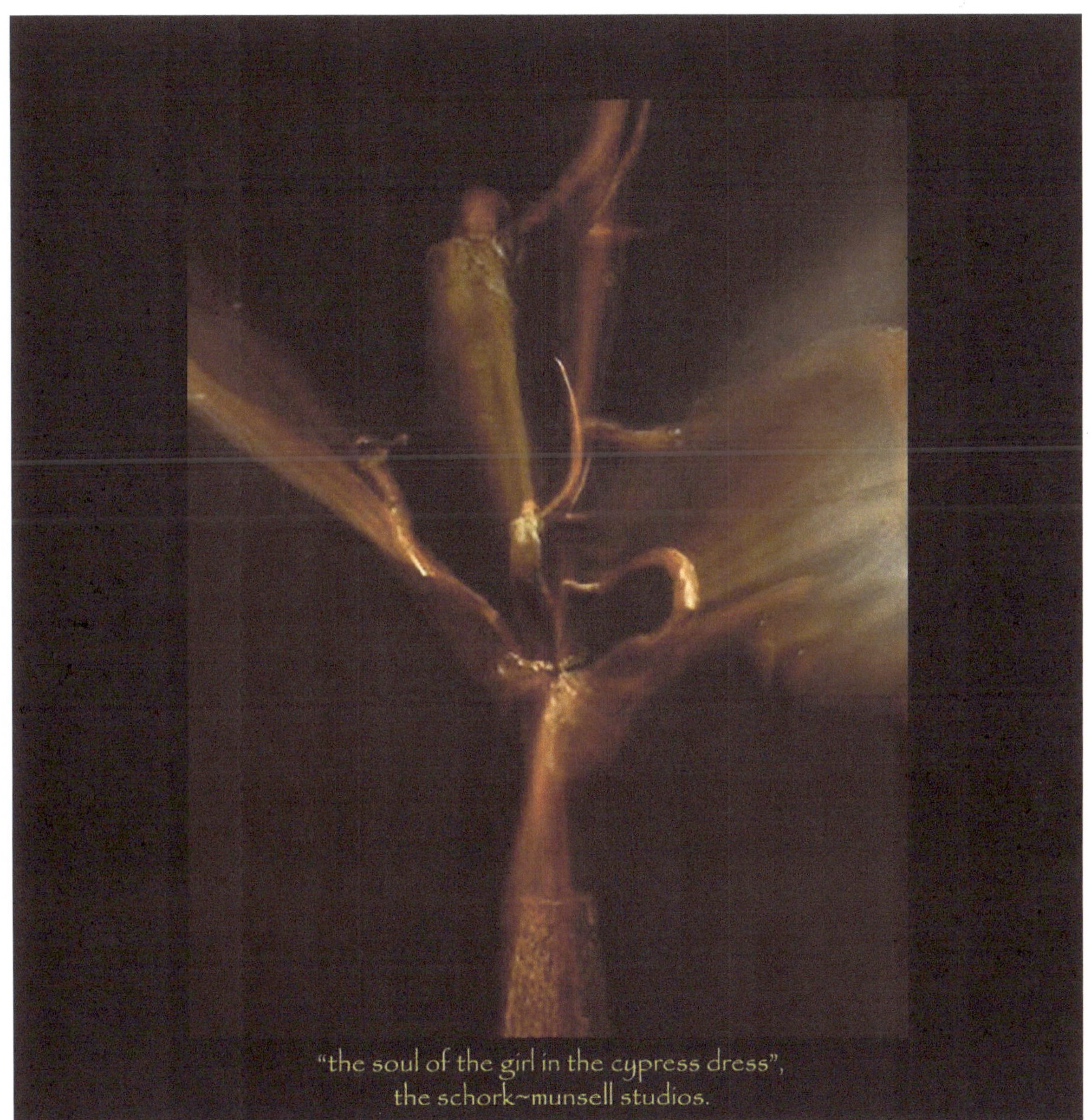

"the soul of the girl in the cypress dress",
the schork~munsell studios.

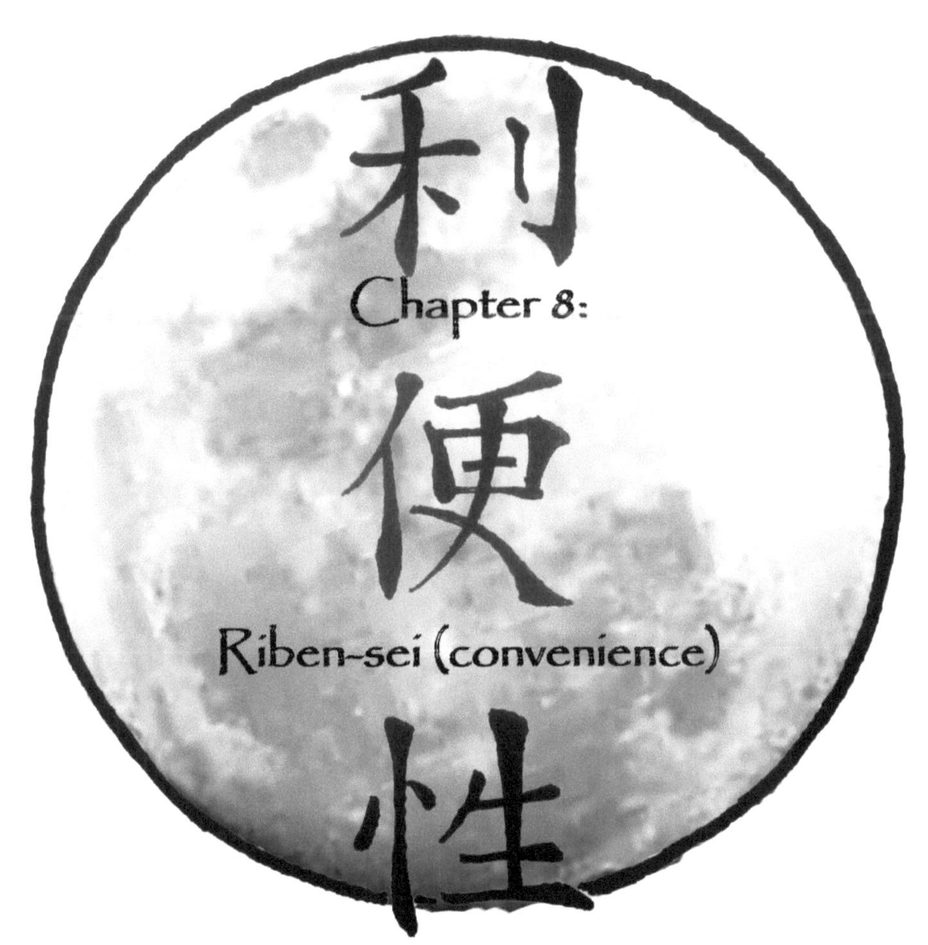
利
Chapter 8:
便
Riben-sei (convenience)
性

Convenience, part 1:

"Matters of convenience are like the fruit that falls to the ground:

it is ripe, but one shares it with the worms."

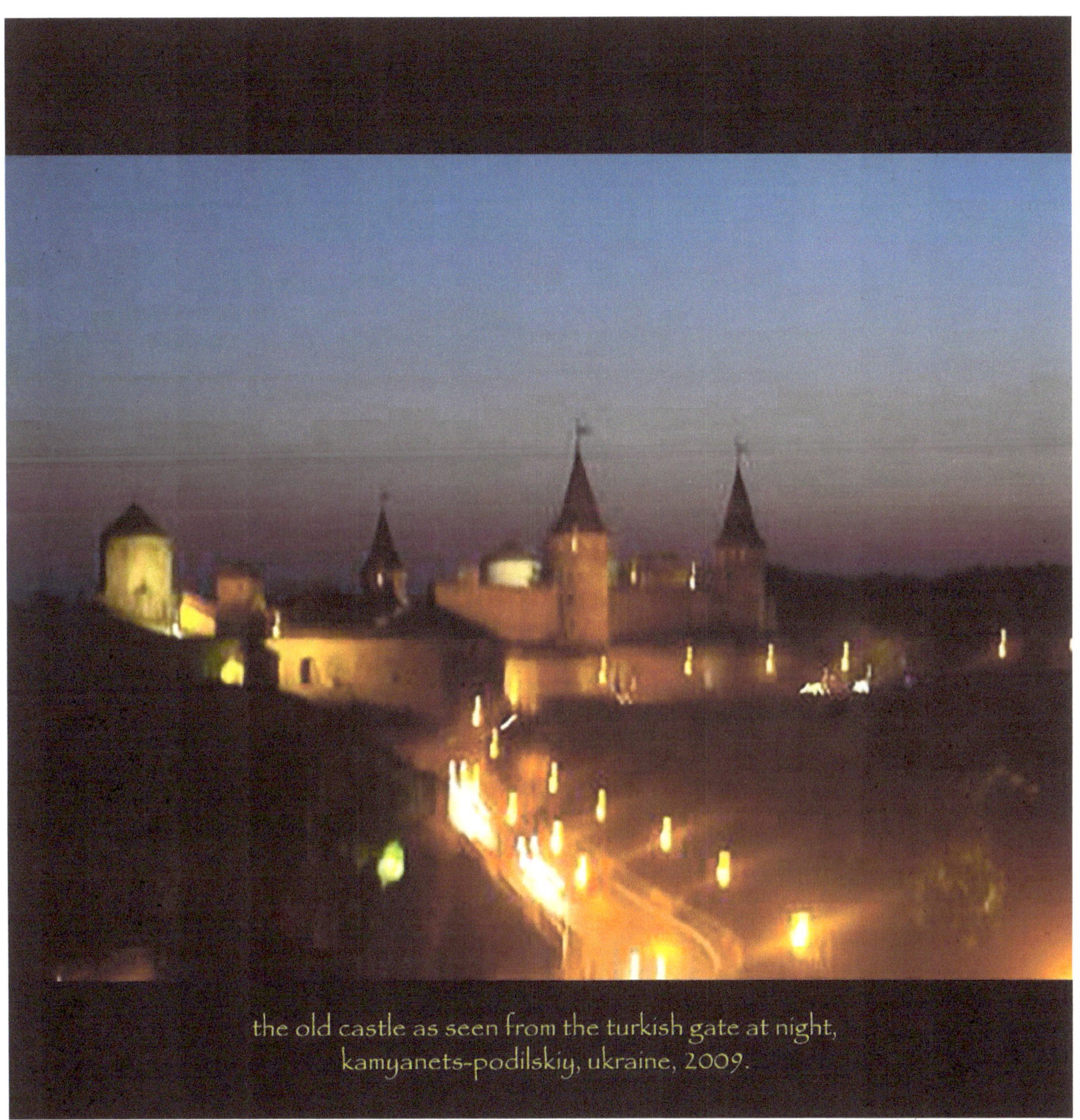

the old castle as seen from the turkish gate at night,
kamyanets-podilskiy, ukraine, 2009.

Convenience, part 2:

"Things that are inconvenient may require that you climb the tree,

but the fruit is fresh & the view is better from up there."

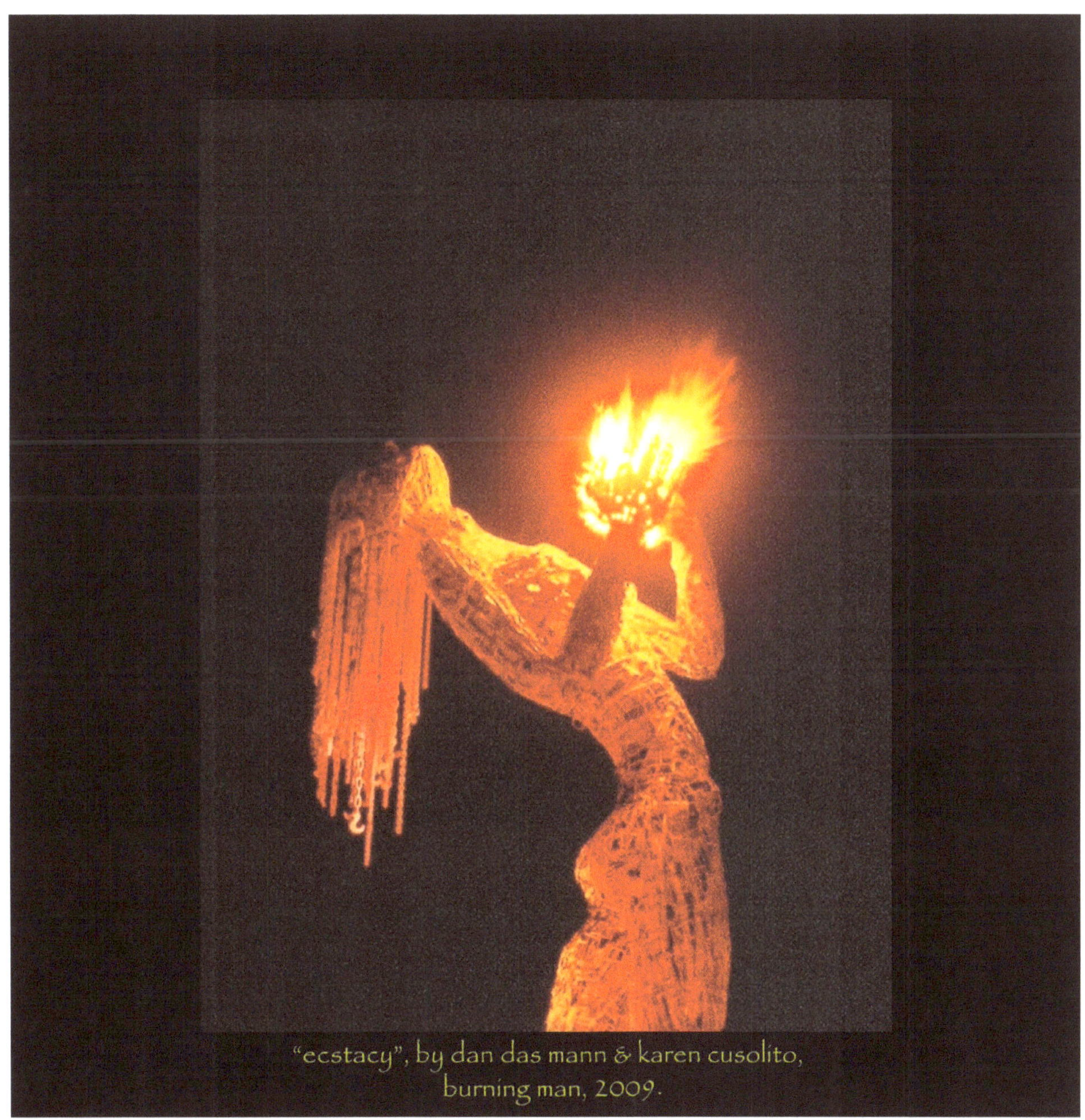

"ecstacy", by dan das mann & karen cusolito,
burning man, 2009.

La Descente~

Mon âme las se detacher

Comme une feuille descendit passé

De sa verte perchoir en lair libérer

Dans le chagrin de la gueule d'hiver.

(The descent~

My weary, disconnected soul

Like a leaf downward falls

From its verdant perch aloft released

Into the grief of winter's gaping maw.)

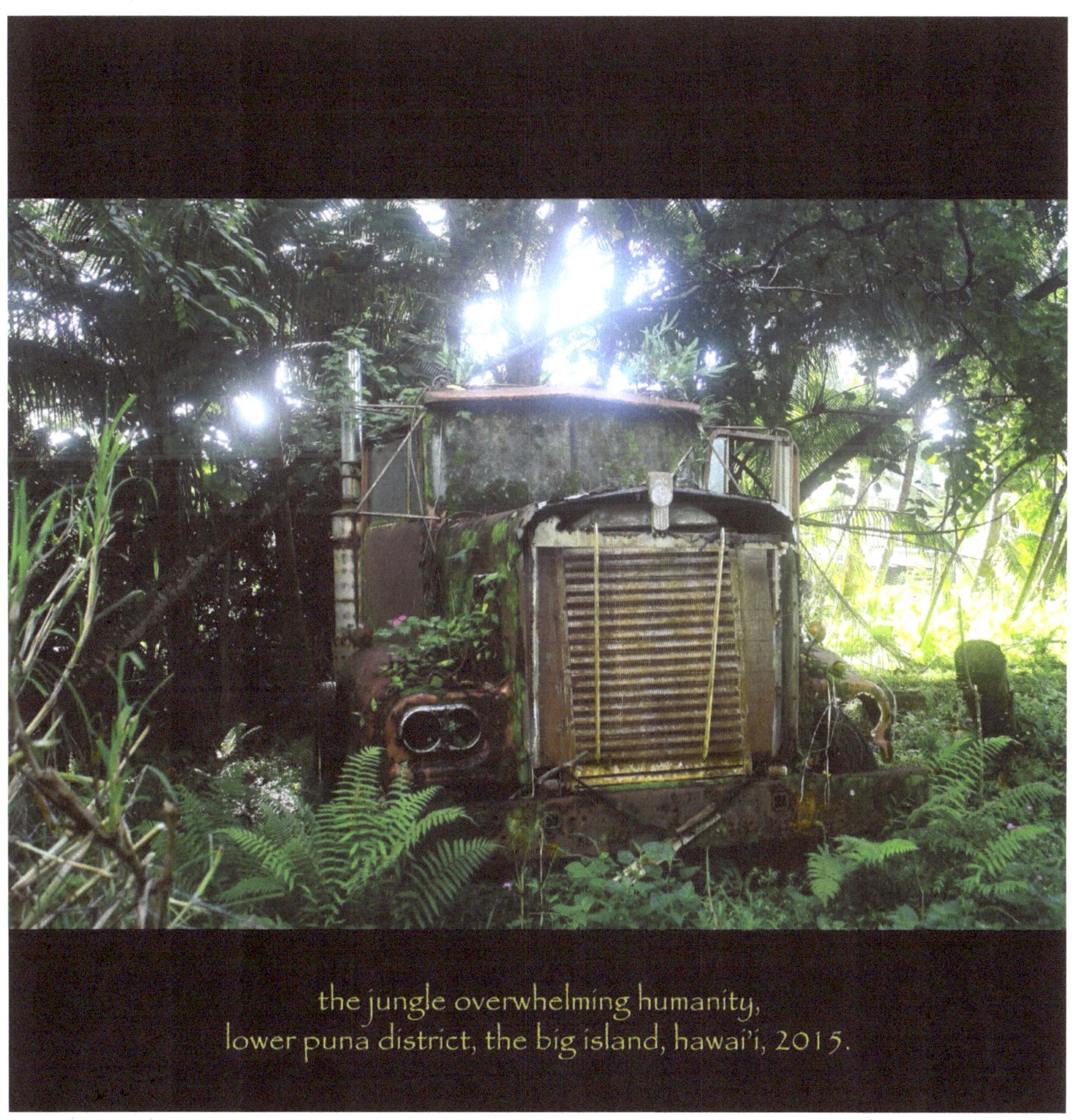

the jungle overwhelming humanity,
lower puna district, the big island, hawai'i, 2015.

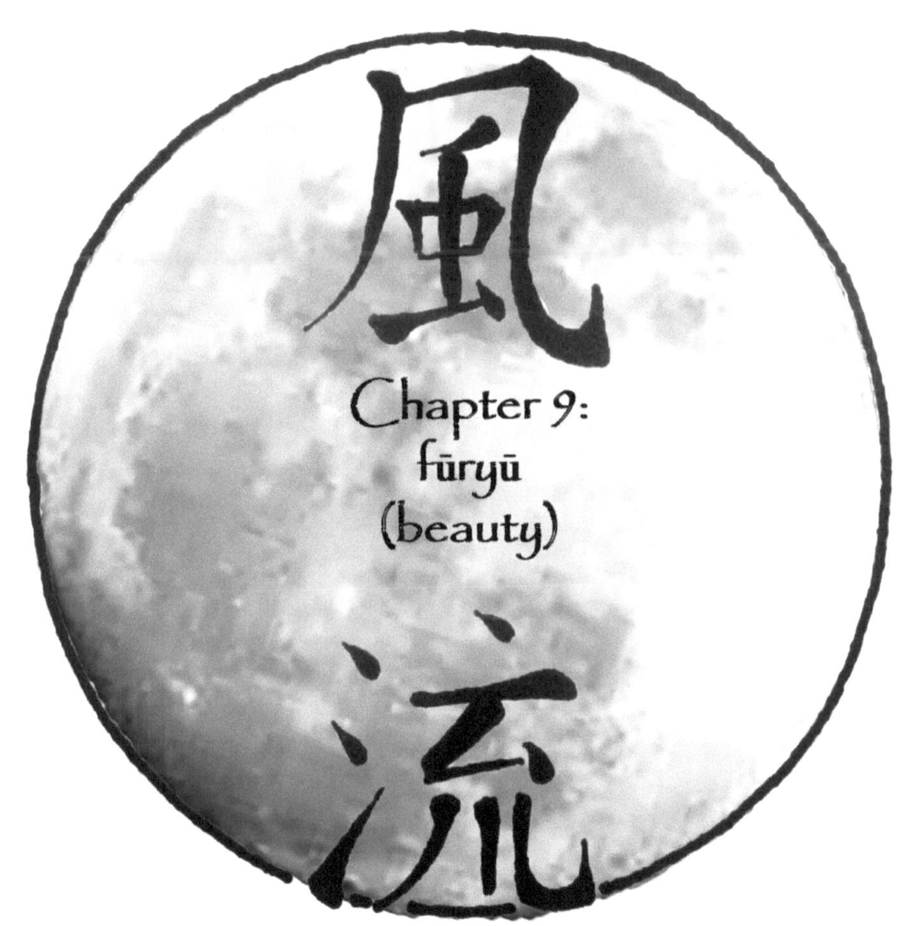
風
Chapter 9:
fūryū
(beauty)
流

Beauty, part 1:

"The world is full of beauty, which requires only that we witness it."

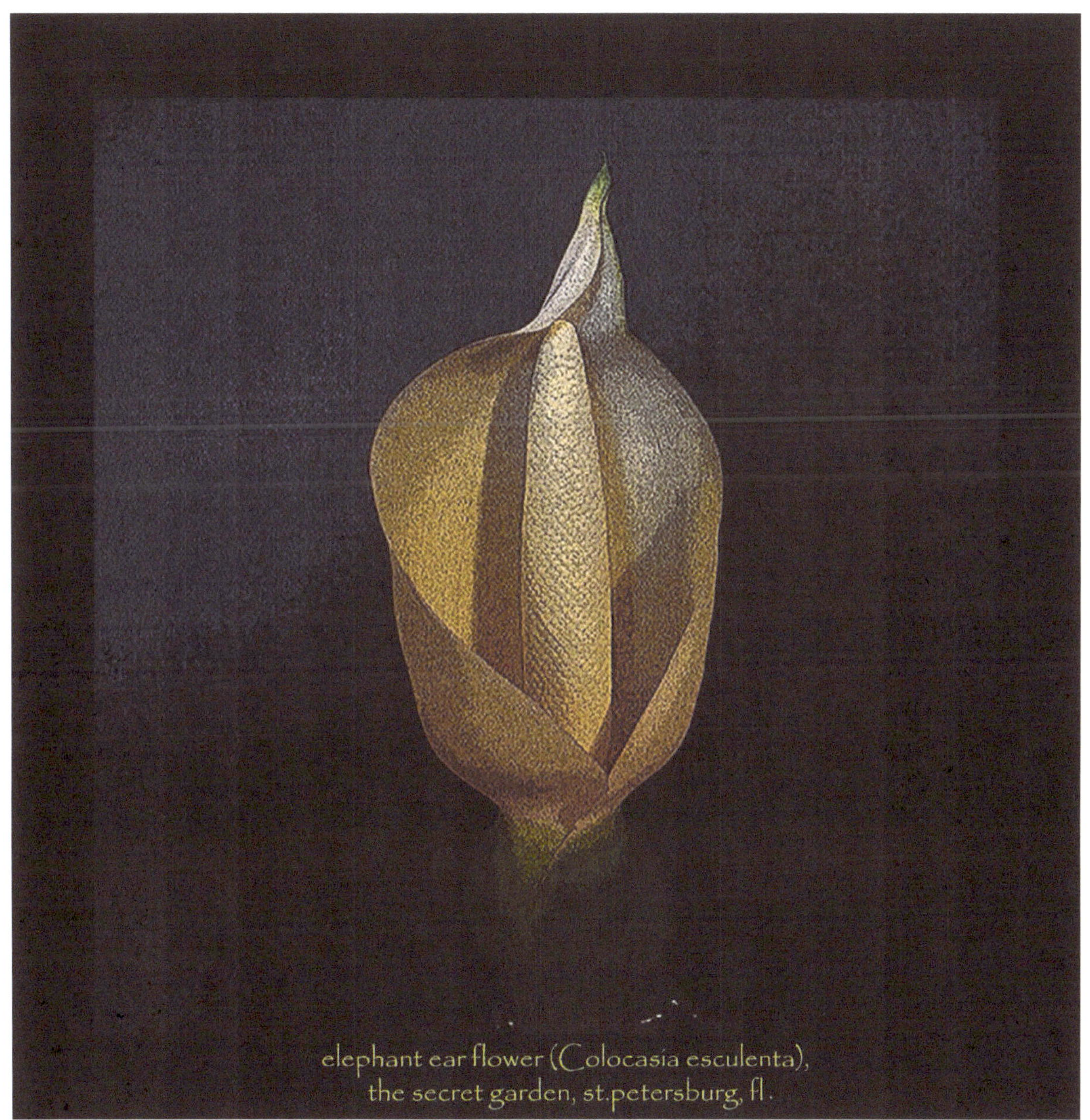
elephant ear flower (Colocasia esculenta),
the secret garden, st.petersburg, fl.

Beauty, part 2:

"If you cannot find beauty, it may be necessary to create it."

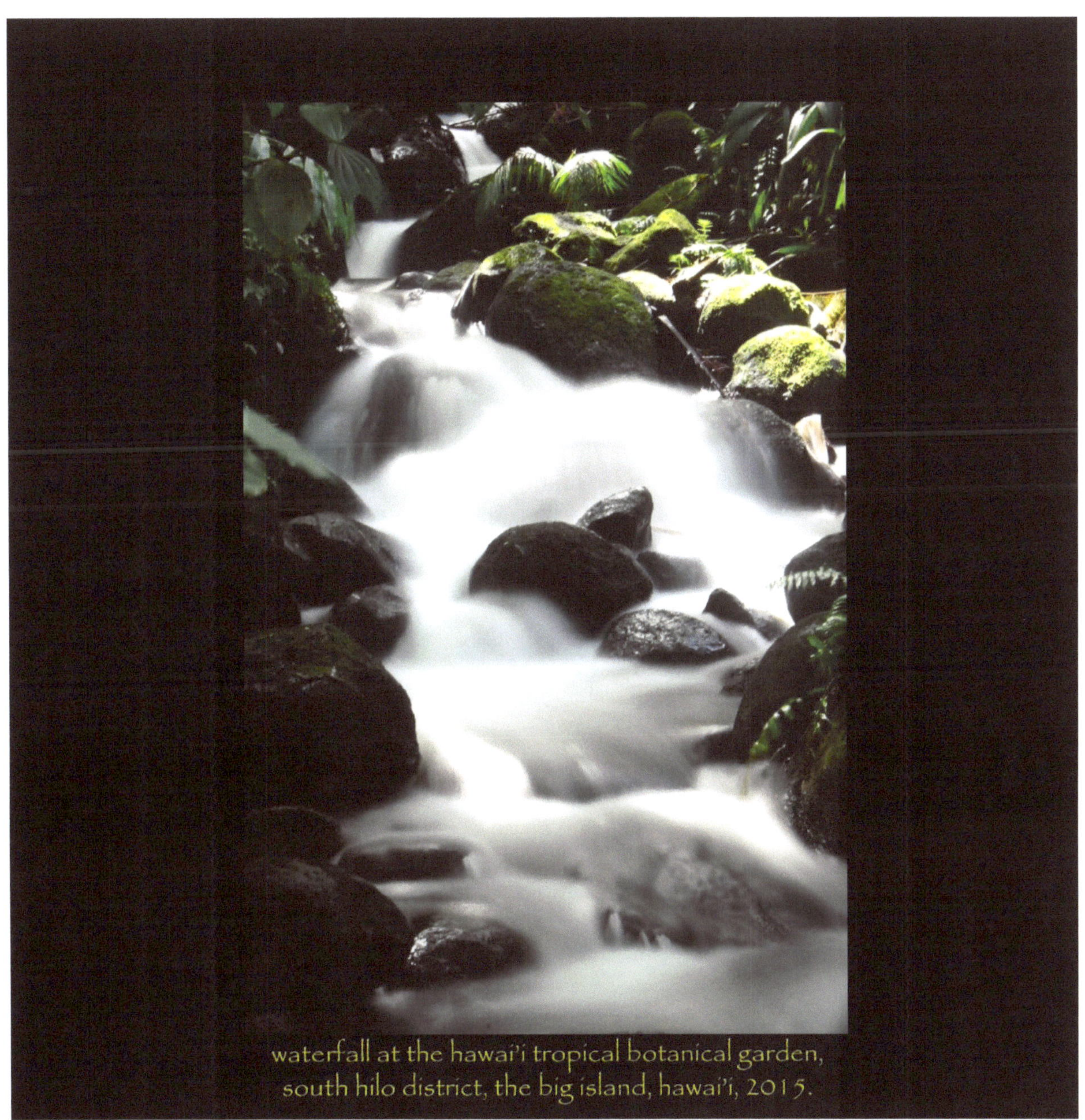

waterfall at the hawai'i tropical botanical garden,
south hilo district, the big island, hawai'i, 2015.

the ladybug with dragon wings

(la coccinelle avec des ailes de dragon)

did you forget me while you slept?   was i lost in that brief slumber?
Lethe in stealth upon you crept: & left me in the dark to wonder.

in the shimmering rain you bring to me...   in the hopeless time between the tears...
i watched your dreams all fade away, amid the torrent of your fears.

to hopelessness my heart you sent   where memories of you reside,
fiercely wild, magnificent, but dragon-wings left still untried.

if i could sing a song of you,
i'd sing away your doubt & pain,
& banish boys who were not true,
& dance with you amid the rain,
& dance until you flew again...

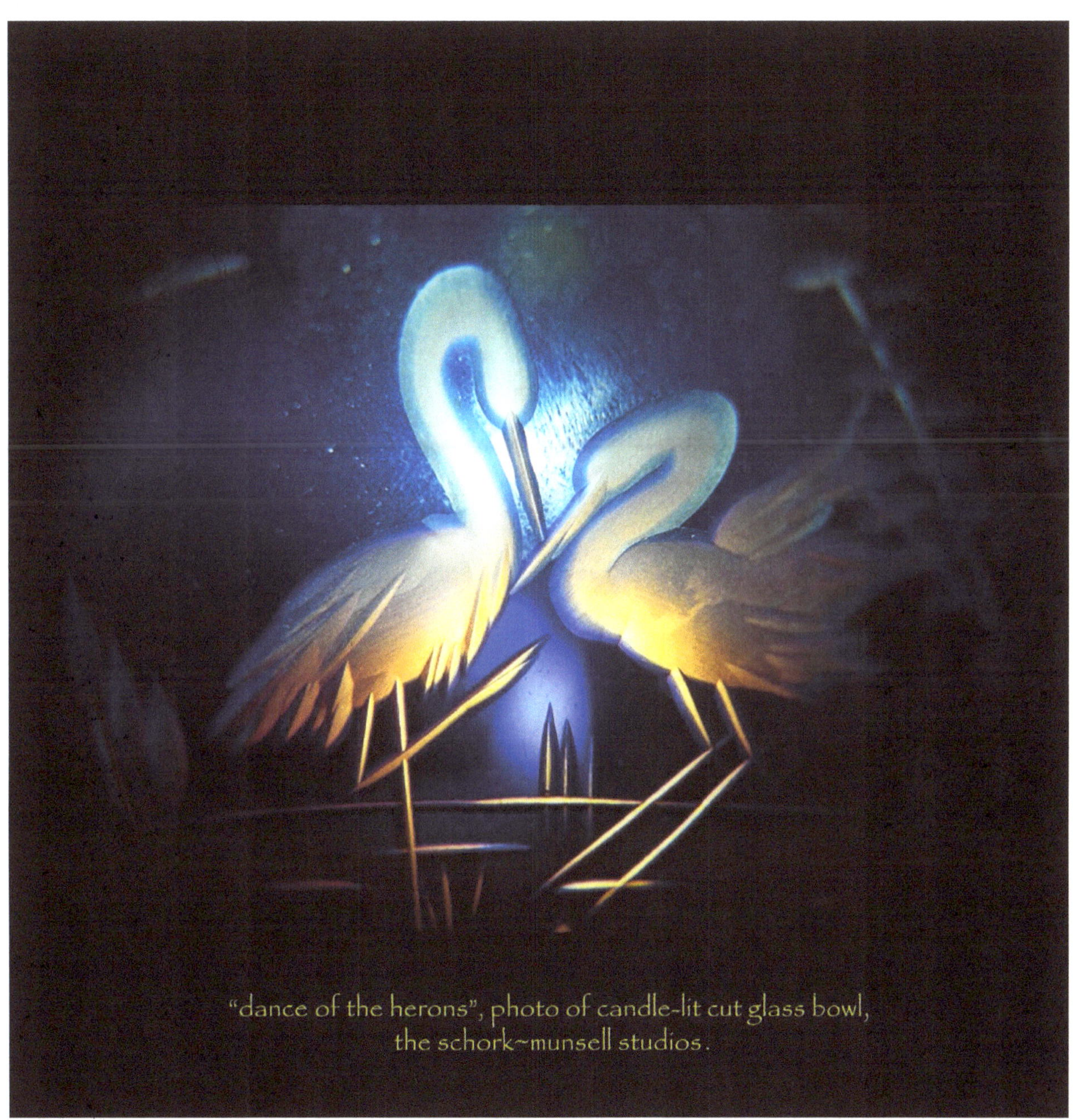

"dance of the herons", photo of candle-lit cut glass bowl,
the schork~munsell studios.

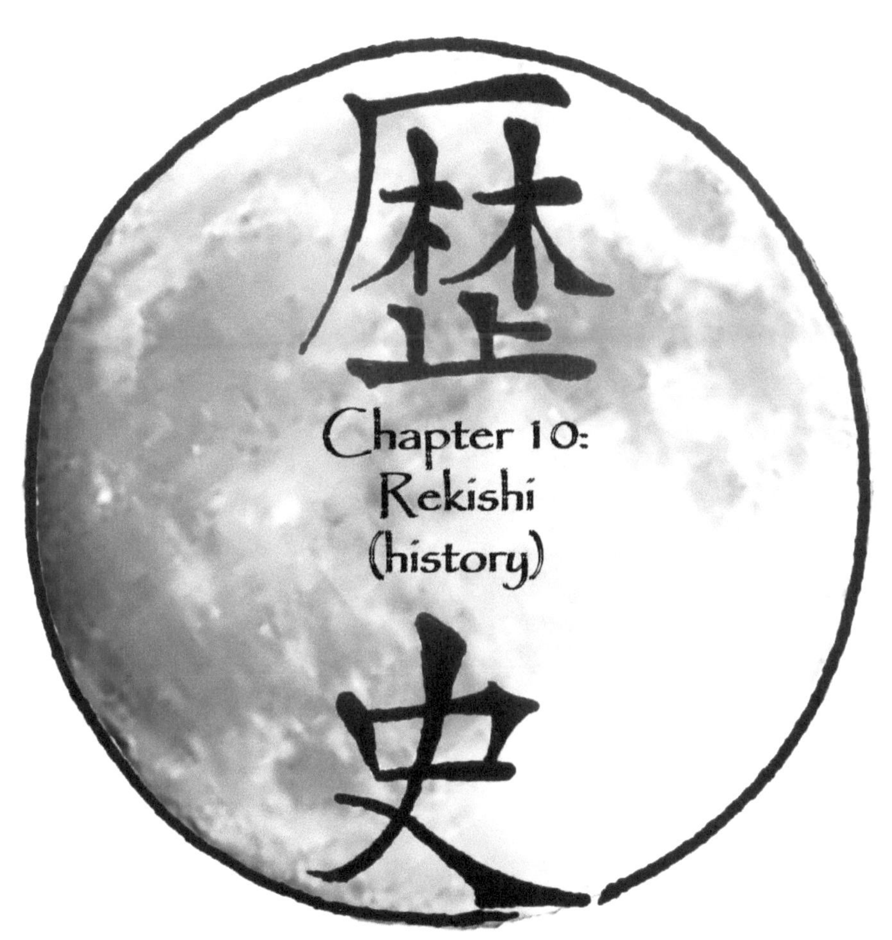
歴
Chapter 10:
Rekishi
(history)
史

History, part 1:

"Each of us has a story, which is every day & every person that has preceded today."

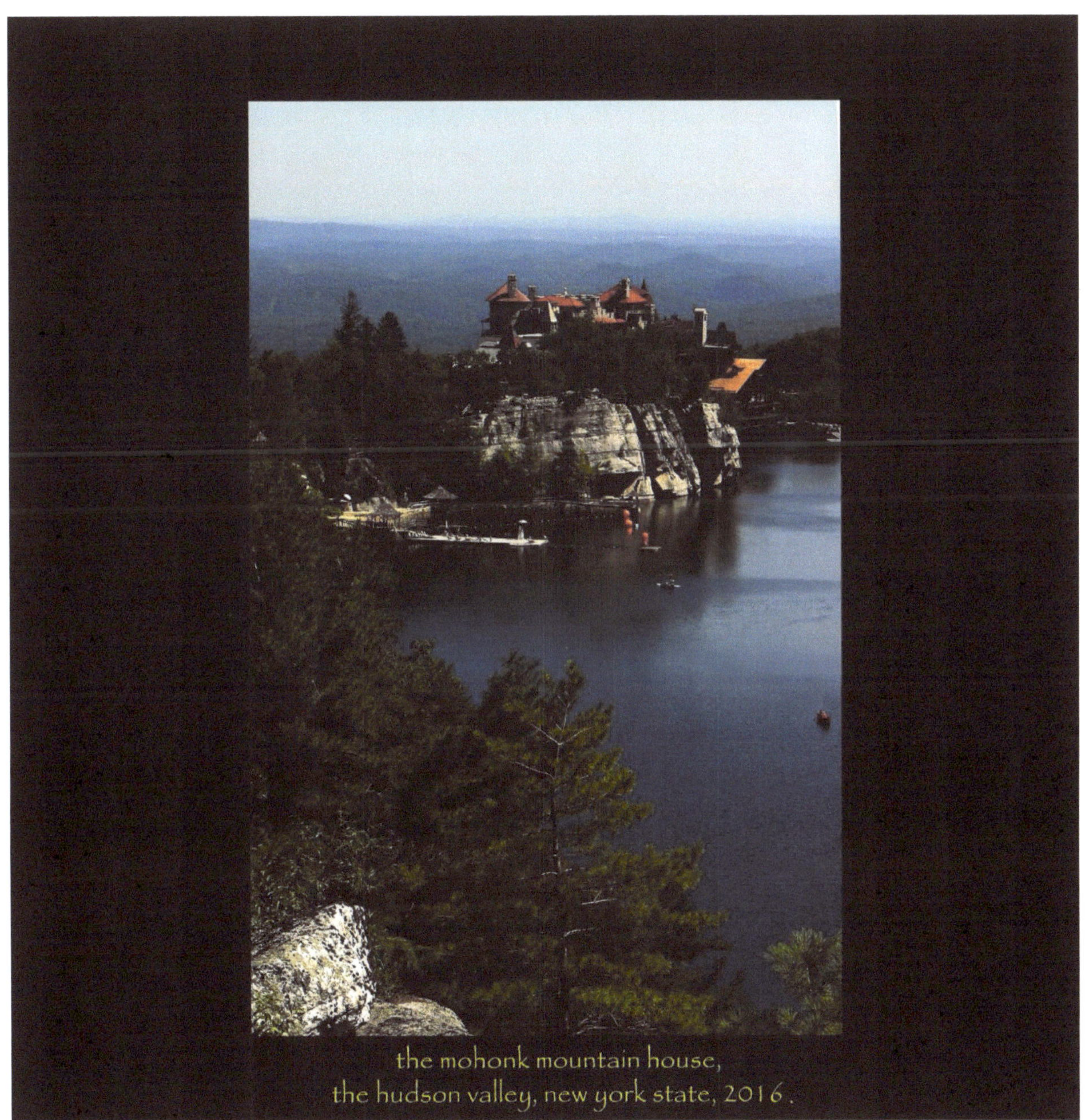

the mohonk mountain house,
the hudson valley, new york state, 2016 .

History, part 2:

"History can become a prison if you forget that it is behind you."

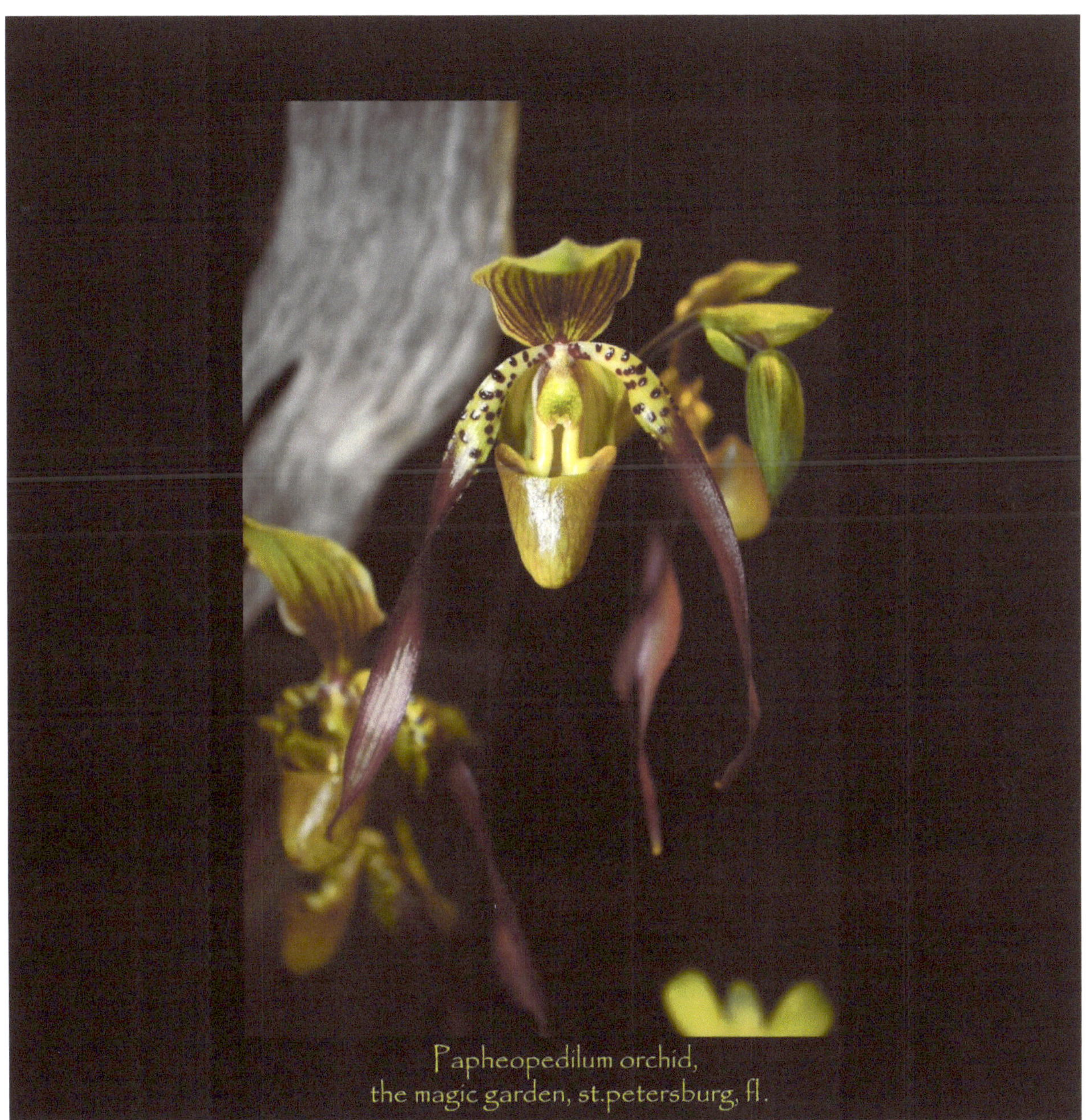

Papheopedilum orchid,
the magic garden, st.petersburg, fl.

Doko kara ka~

O Chocho,

Hana no aijin,

Imomushi omoidesu...

(Whence~

Butterfly,

Mistress of flowers,

Remember caterpillar...)

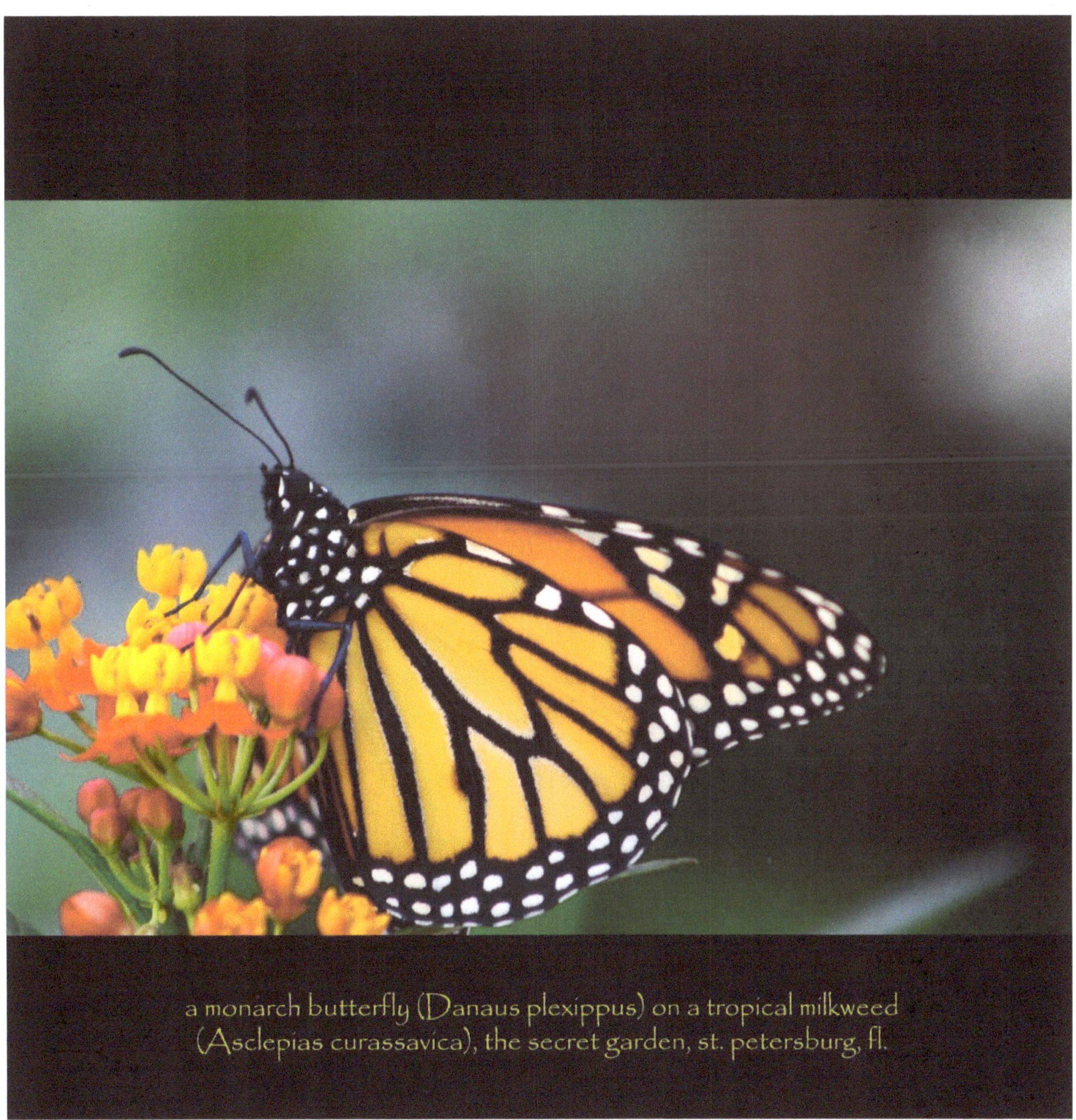

a monarch butterfly (Danaus plexippus) on a tropical milkweed (Asclepias curassavica), the secret garden, st. petersburg, fl.

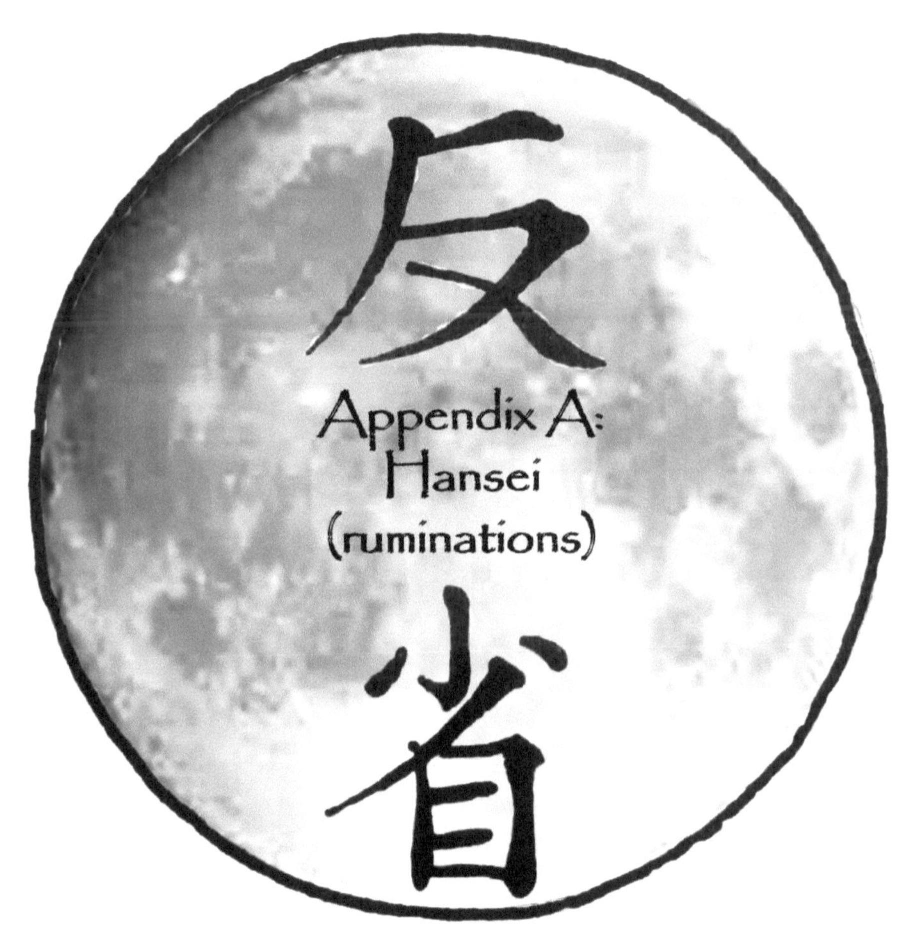
反
Appendix A:
Hansei
(ruminations)
省

Appendix A:

Ruminations,

being the random thoughts that are often, after much reflexion,

refined into tenets...

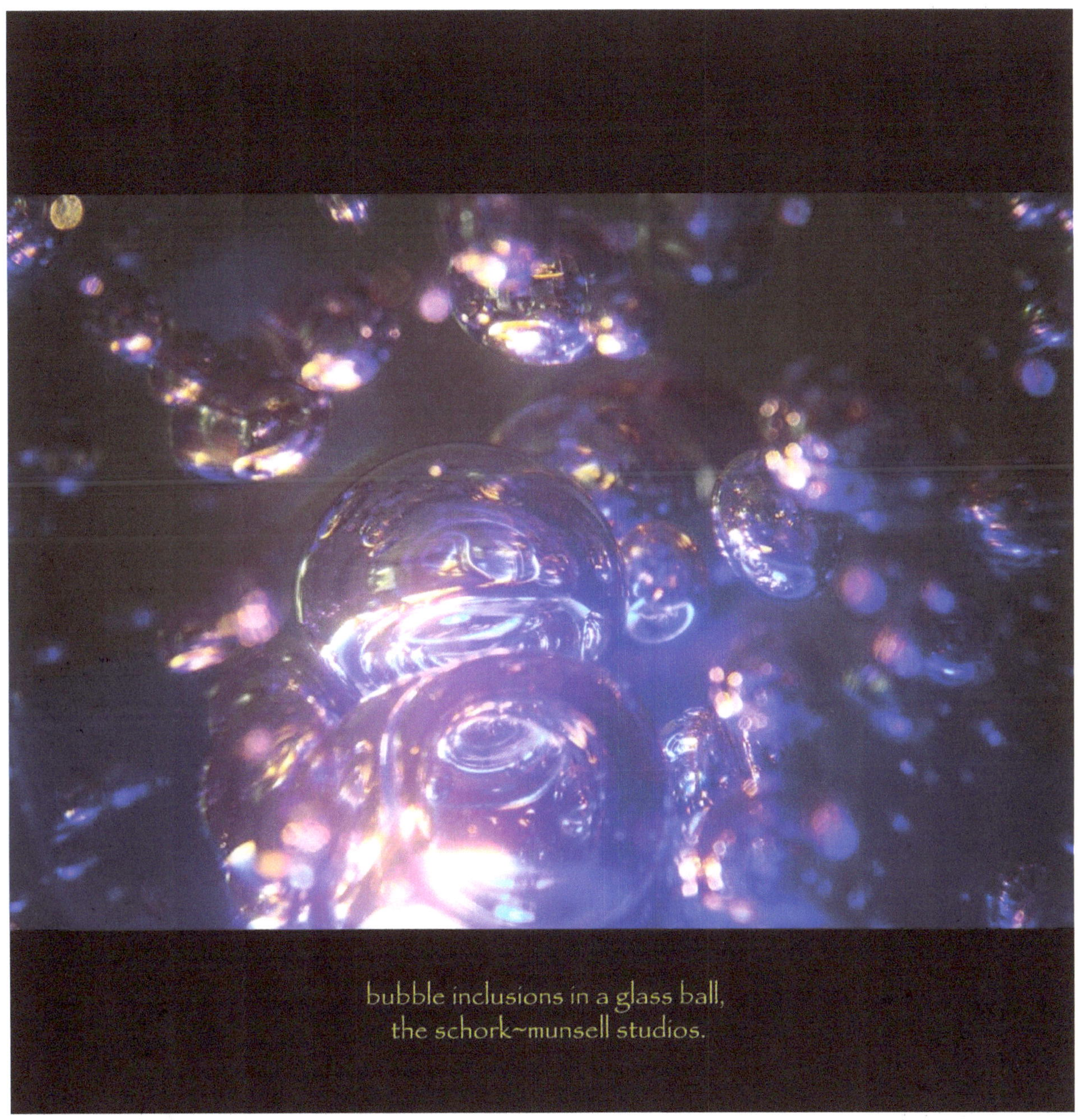

bubble inclusions in a glass ball,
the schork~munsell studios.

On fairness:

Life is not a matter of fairness; it is a matter of endurance.

Some of us are made to endure much more than others.

If one is unable to endure, one either sadly succumbs,

or one resorts to the baser impulses of our species—

the instruments of selfishness that make life unfair.

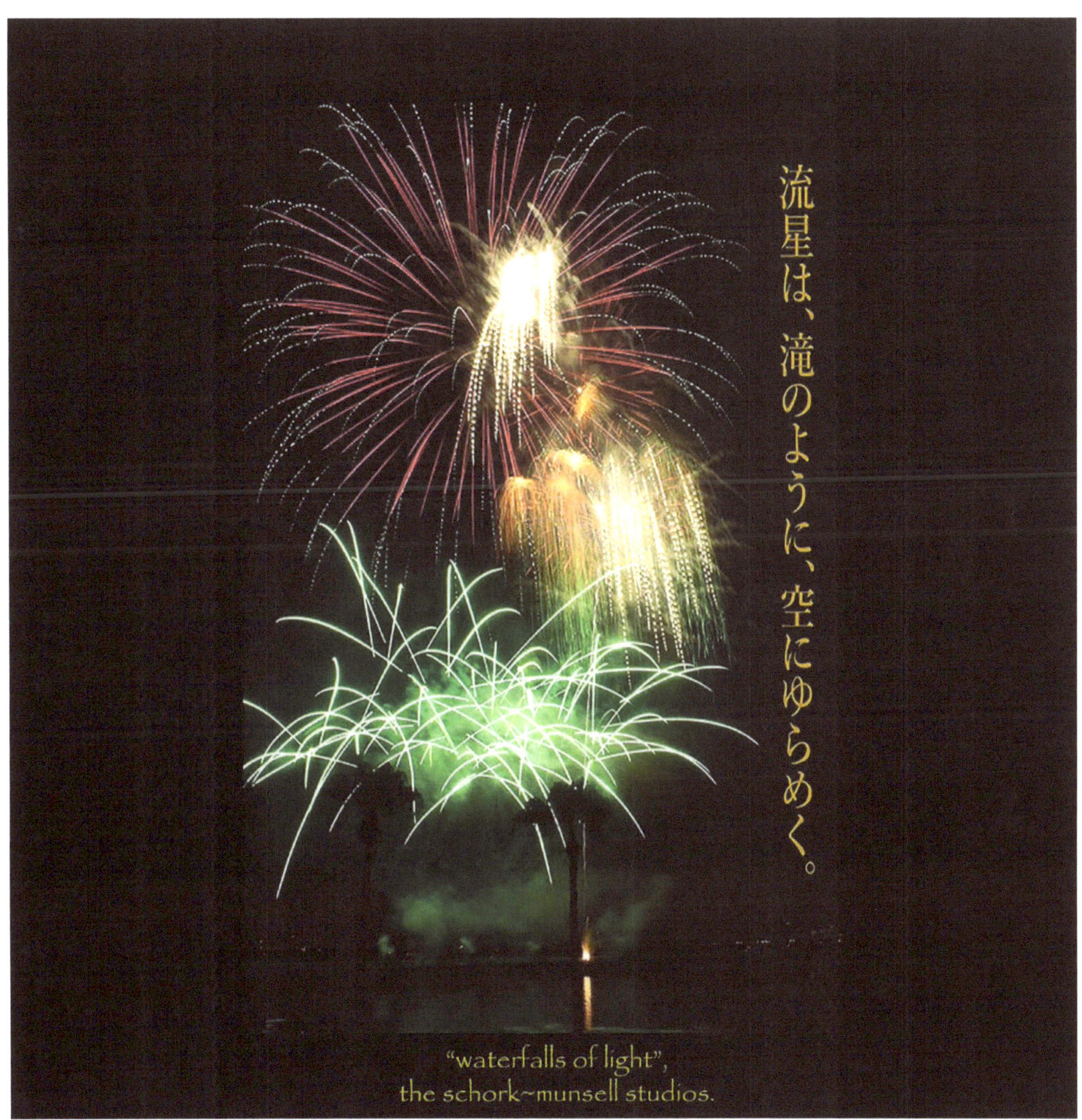

"waterfalls of light",
the schork~munsell studios.

On travel, & the habits of wanderers:

The best way to learn about your house is to visit houses that are not yours. To travel is not merely a luxury: Joseph Campbell's hero makes his journey to return to his village with treasures for all the people who will never leave it. What are these treasures? They are new foods, new words, new tools & ideas, new friends, & the wisdom to understand their value. This is why we wander...

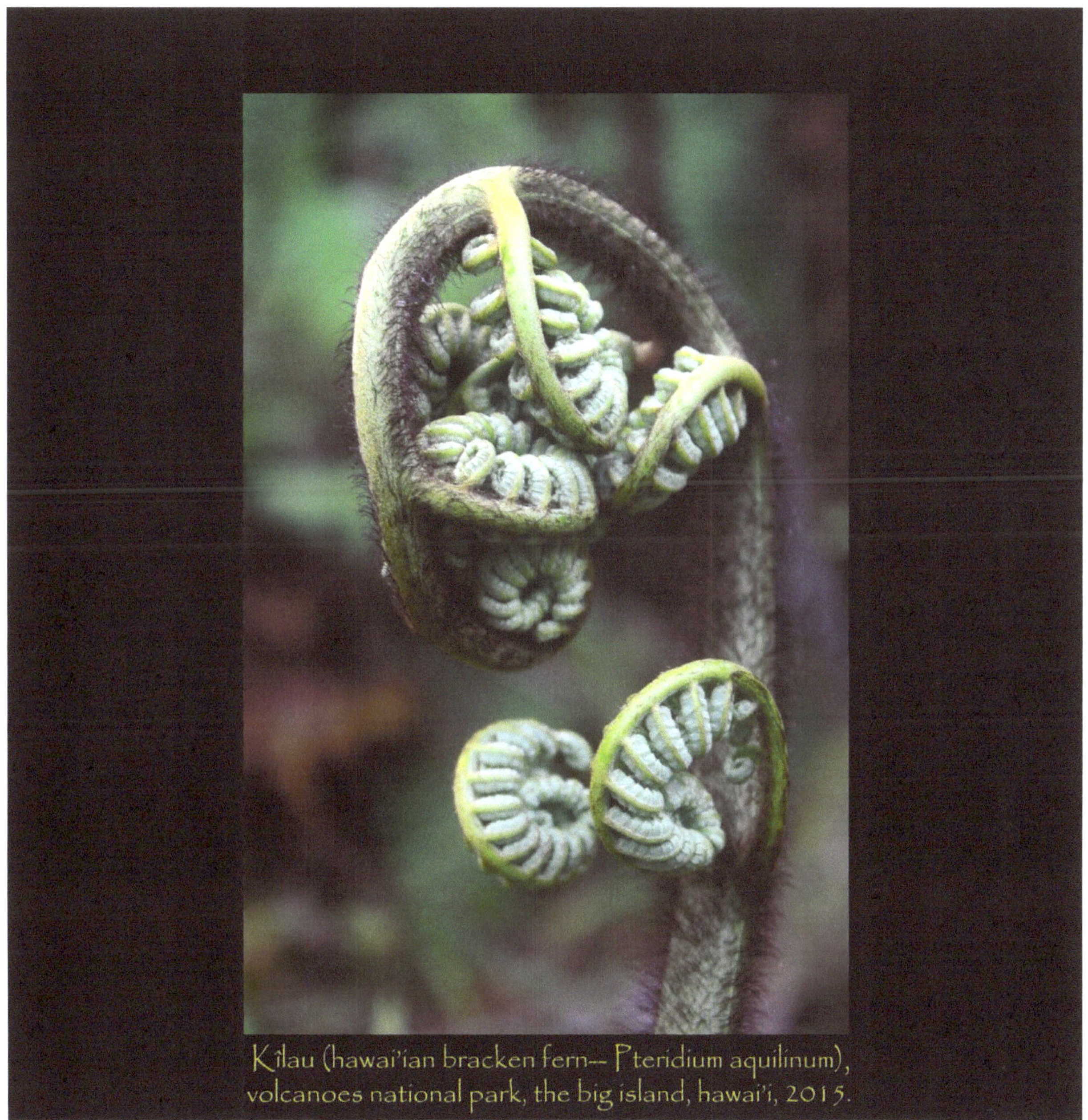

Kîlau (hawai’ian bracken fern-- Pteridium aquilinum),
volcanoes national park, the big island, hawai’i, 2015.

On exile:

Everything has a beginning & an end, not least our relationships. We have a propensity—many of us—perhaps to want to linger longer than we should in a place we have worn out. It is an expression of courage & self-respect to leave when leaving has been ordained for us, it matters not by whom, nor why. Our place is not to instruct the world in the errors of exiling us; there is an intrinsic beauty in willingly donning the rags of the leper: they are the costume for our part in the ridiculous farces of others...

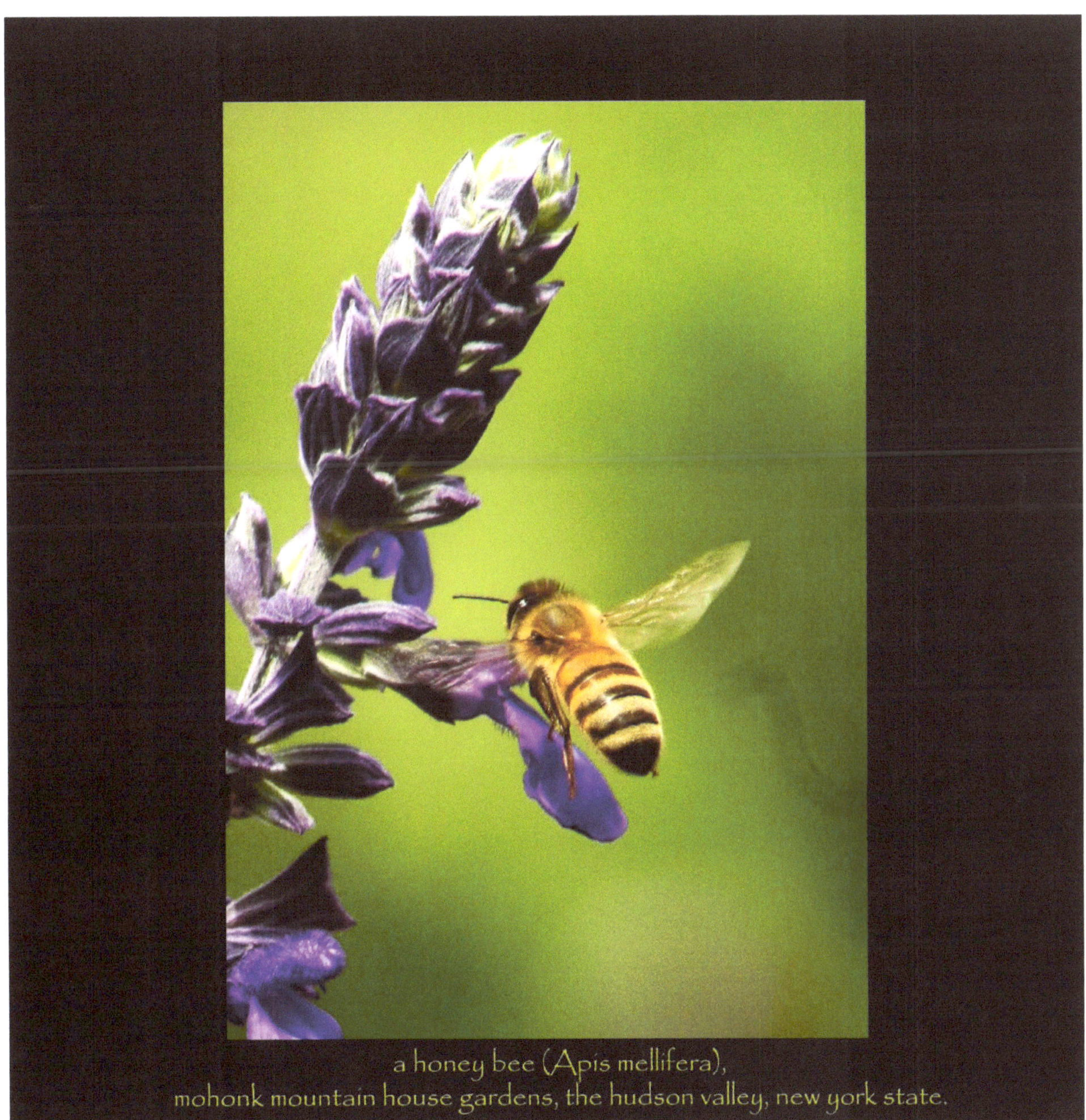

a honey bee (Apis mellifera),
mohonk mountain house gardens, the hudson valley, new york state.

On being:

Tough times reveal the best & worst of us: courage or cowardice, kindness or cruelty, generosity or greed, the polite or the rude, the smart or the stupid. Whom do you want to be?

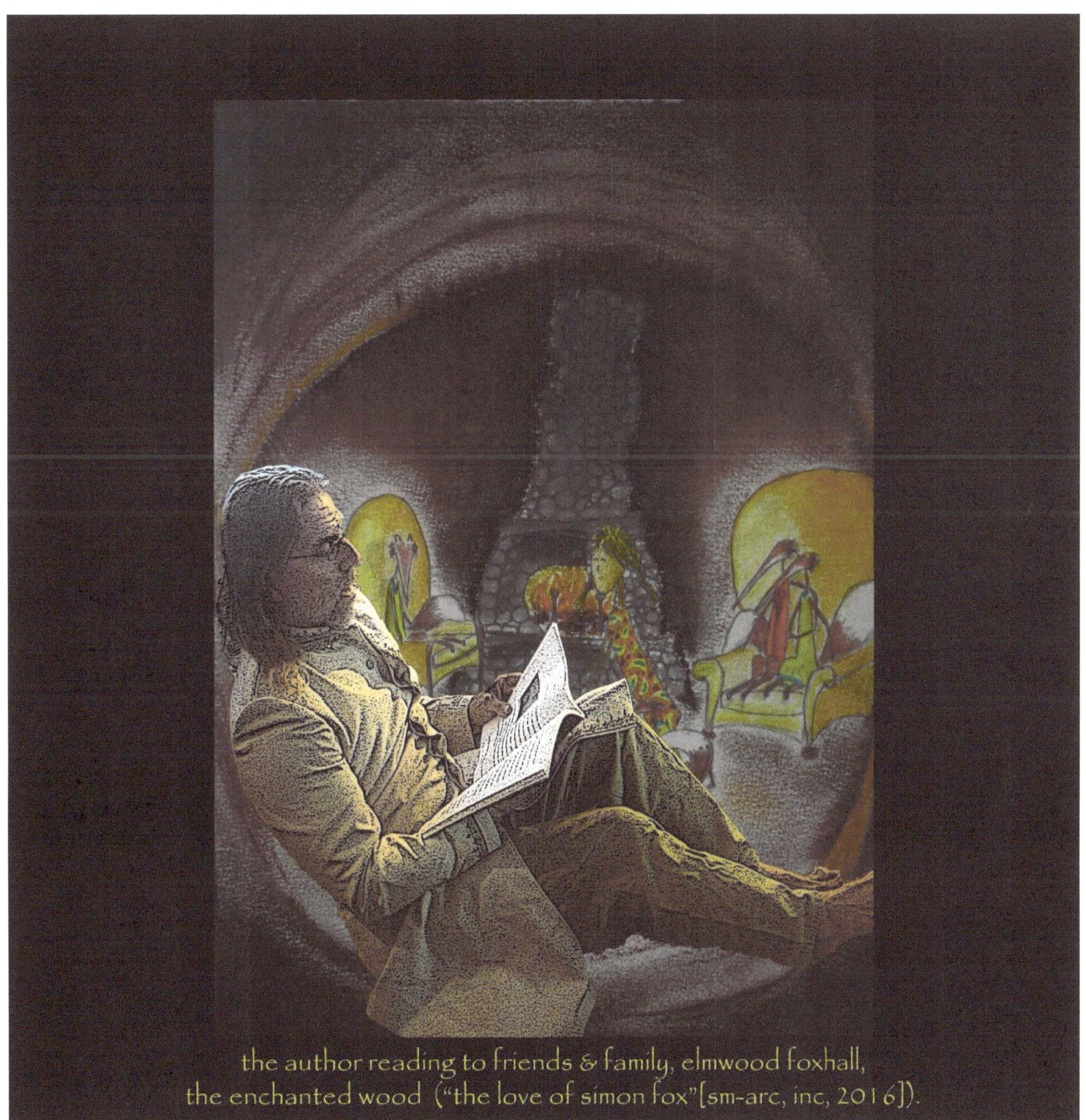

the author reading to friends & family, elmwood foxhall,
the enchanted wood ("the love of simon fox"[sm-arc, inc, 2016]).

www.ingramcontent.com/pod-product-compliance
Lightning Source LLC
LaVergne TN
LVHW070133110826
845147LV00002B/241
9780997921205